HOPES
AND FEARS

HOPES
AND FEARS

The Human Future

Edited by Hanna Newcombe

Canadian Papers in Peace Studies
1992 No. 2

Science for Peace / Samuel Stevens
Toronto
1992

Science for Peace is a Canadian charitable corporation, registered in Ontario, funded by membership subscriptions, and by individual and corporate donations. Its objectives include encouragement of research and education for peace, as well as for the abolition of weapons of mass destruction.

Science for Peace
University College
University of Toronto
Toronto, Ontario M5S 1A1

Samuel Stevens & Co.
University of Toronto Press
5201 Dufferin Street
Downsview, Ontario M3H 5T8
Canada

Canadian Cataloguing in Publication Data

Main entry under title:

Hopes and fears: the human future

(Canadian papers in peace studies)
Includes bibliographical references.
ISBN 0-88866-950-X

1. International cooperation. 2. Security, International. 3. Environmental protection — international cooperation. I. Newcombe, Hanna, 1922-
II. Science for Peace (Association)

D2009.H66 1992   327.1'7   C92-094335-7

Printed in Canada

ACKNOWLEDGEMENTS

This book is sponsored by the World Federal Authority Committee, a small international research group affiliated to the World Federalist Movement.

We wish to thank the Lannung Foundation in Copenhagen for a grant that made this book possible, and Pat Woodcock for invaluable help in its production.

Hanna Newcombe
Peace Research Institute, Dundas
February 1, 1992

CONTENTS

IV. VALUES AND COOPERATION

V. ECOLOGICAL ISSUES

INTRODUCTION

It has been said many times that the human future is clouded by multiple and mutually interacting problems. While in the 19th century we had the luxury of believing in almost automatic progress – an "onward and upward" assumption – that belief has been shattered by two world wars, more than 150 smaller ones, the invention of weapons of mass destruction, increasing degradation of the environment, both by pollution and resource exhaustion (i.e. adding "bads" and subtracting "goods" from our natural endowment), a horrendous (and increasing) gap between rich and poor within and between nations, explosions of racism and chauvinistic nationalism, increasing use of torture as a police method, totalitarian regimes, repeated episodes of genocide . . . not a picture of progress toward a better world. And yet, we have not quite lost faith in the human potential for more beneficial and harmonious development. We know that we could do much better, that we are adaptable and resourceful and capable of learning from mistakes, that science has progressed and can (if we so apply it) better our lot. Moreover, the more gifted among us have produced great works of literature, art, music, and theatre, which it would be a pity to lose. We have an investment in our own continuation, if it can be managed – if we foreswear the use of our weapons, and reach a tacit agreement with nature so as to pass her rigorous tests for survival. The authors of this collection address these fears and hopes in various ways and differing styles.

The issues addressed are all related to peace in the larger sense. In the section on *War Prevention*, this is very direct: non-offensive defence (Fischer) and verification (Scott and Dorn) deal with arms and arms control. *Future Scenarios for Europe* is a section discussing the post-Cold-War world, which is the necessary political complement to disarmament in that region and which has been the centre of fears about nuclear war. *Global Decision Making* will be a necessary aspect of a world governed jointly by all the nations and peoples; international law and the United Nations (reformed in various ways) will be key factors in this. Values for peace and cooperation will require profound changes in psychology and ethics if peace is to be achieved, and the essays in this section address the problems from an inter-disciplinary point of view. Finally, ecological issues cannot be ignored; their connections to peace issues have been pointed out many times, e.g. ecological damage caused by war, conflict over resources as a cause of war, and cross-border pollution problems.

This is a book on problems and solutions. It is necessary, but not sufficient, to state the problems; proposals for solving them must accompany such statements, or our fears will overpower our hopes. The solutions proposed here will, no doubt, not be the ones finally adopted; but they may at least point the way and stimulate fruitful discussion. It is in this spirit that we offer this collection of essays.

With events moving very rapidly in 1991, when this book was being edited, some of the essays may be somewhat out of date, as has been the fate of many other books and articles this year. Rather than taking the time for a complete up-date, we decided to publish now, and simply caution the reader to remember that the time of writing of some of the essays was late 1990 or early 1991. Several authors, Arnold Simoni and Bjørn Møller, have kindly up-dated their contributions in record short time, for which we are very thankful.

HOPES
AND FEARS

PART I. — FUTURE SCENARIOS FOR EUROPE

A Common Security System for Europe?

BJØRN MØLLER*

The Nineties According To Heraclitus

The pre-Socratic Greek philosopher Heraclitus of Ephesus (ca. 540-480 B.C.) might serve as our spiritual guide in our quest for comprehending the present and future situation in Europe. He is, above all, known for his phrase "panta rei" ("all things are in process" or "everything is moving")[1] which admirably sums up the most distinguishing feature of the present. The prevalent state of flux and increased turbulence is partly, but not merely, a result of the 1989 revolutions in Eastern Europe and the resultant collapse of communism. Whereas the "old" systemic conflict has thus been turned into a thing of the past, its successor as the "ordering principle" of international relations has not yet become apparent, although potential candidates are already appearing on the stage: The future might be shaped by either of the following dichotomies, or any combination thereof: North/South, occidental/oriental, Christian/Muslim, land power/sea power, or nationalism/ globalism.

Trends And Dangers

Unless otherwise indicated, the following account merely refers to "Europe" (including both superpowers only in as far as their relations with "Europe proper" are concerned), i.e. what might

---

* Extracts from Working Papers (6/1990), originally written for a seminar in Moscow.

be called "CSCE Europe" (Conference on Security and Cooperation in Europe; for other such abbreviations, see the Glossary in Appendix A at end of this chapter, p. 30). The rest of the globe is largely disregarded.

It has been impossible to take into account the dissolution of the USSR. Whether the Confederation Russia, Ukraine and Byelorussia will constitute a genuine succession remains to be seen, but seems at least possible. References to "the two super-powers" should be seen in this light.

Military Trends

1. *The nuclear arms control process (INF, START, etc.) may soon accomplish a fifty percent reduction in strategic nuclear arms, only to be followed by further cuts.* Both superpowers have proclaimed 50 percent reductions of strategic nuclear arms to be their objective for the START negotiations[2], although the treaty actually concluded amounts to only about 30 percent. One reason for this encouraging development may be that, even if these cuts exceeded 50 percent, both superpowers would remain comfortably within the "overkill range", and still remote from the point where the "marginal destructive utility" of any increment to the arsenals declines steeply. Thus, even deep cuts would only affect the aggregate destructive potential to a marginal extent.

2. *The British and French nuclear weapons may remain outside the strategic arms reduction talks.* Until now, neither the UK nor France have shown any willingness whatsoever to place their strategic weapons on the negotiating table. Furthermore, both states are involved in an ambitious expansion-cum-modernization programme (including extensive "MIRV-ing") which may, at best, be slowed down somewhat due to economic constraints[3]. Only in the UK, moreover, would a change of government significantly change this direction.

3. *The credibility of nuclear first-use may continue to decline, approaching zero.* Owing to trend 1 (above) and to both

superpowers' acknowledgement (made e.g. at the Reykjavik summit) that "a nuclear war must never be fought", the credibility of nuclear deterrent threats may have become almost nil, especially in so far as "extended deterrence" is concerned, i.e. when it is a question of opting for a (most likely suicidal) nuclear war for the sake of less than "existential" interests[4]. Some would further argue (although the present author would disagree) that the first-use option has been sacrificed by the arms control cuts in the "theatre range" (the INF treaty), and that it may be further impeded by any reductions in (or, indeed, by an abolition of) the short-range and battlefield categories of nuclear arms.

4. *The conventional forces have been built down to lower numbers, with the brunt of the reductions falling on old-fashioned equipment and manpower.* The CFE Treaty signed in 1990 produced fairly substantial cut-backs, although the brunt of the reductions fell on WTO (and above all Soviet) forces, whereas NATO was obliged to make only marginal reductions. The unilateral reductions undertaken by the USSR and its former allies point in the same direction. However, in the US as well, there are clear indications of a downward turn, reflecting a return to the traditional Republican "balanced budget" philosophy, which necessitates reductions in military expenditures, in their turn only attainable through cutting general-purpose forces.

The first stage of CFE implies, in addition to major reductions, also "equal ceilings" (even though the question "between whom" has arisen as a result of the collapse at the Eastern bloc), thus amounting to the establishment of numerical parity with regard to conventional forces in Europe. From this vantage point further reductions would seem to be realistic as a longer-term perspective.

5. *The technological arms race may continue unabated, and the resultant innovations may emphasize lethality, precision and*

range. There are only a few indications of a halt to the military Research and Development (R&D) momentum, and no curtailment whatsoever of the underlying propellants[5]. Furthermore, for as long as the future appears uncertain, a continuance of the R&D efforts will most likely be perceived as a prudent "hedging of one's bets".

With regard to the direction of the "technological push", one of the main beneficiaries of innovations in weapons technology has up to the present been lethality, which has been increased through the invention of Fuel Air Explosives, scatterable minelets, etc.[6]. Precision has been emphasized as well, and tends to become nearly independent of firing range due to the introduction of guidance systems integral to the weapons themselves. It has thus become possible to increase the range of weapons without this having serious negative implications for their precision[7].

6. *Present trends towards more offensive strategic conceptions may continue, whilst the concurrent opposite trends may come to a halt.* The available evidence is ambiguous. On the one hand, the military strategy, operational art and tactics of the USSR until very recently developed in the offensive direction in several respects. On the other hand, in the Gorbachev era, these trends have been reversed, above all politically, with the support lent to the notions of Non-Offensive Defence (NOD) by the highest Soviet authorities[8], but also to a certain extent materially, by a piecemeal reduction of the most offensive-capable elements of the Soviet posture (cf. the December 1988 announcement in the UN) [9].

As far as the West is concerned the trends seem to point more unambiguously in the offensive direction, albeit from a more defensive vantage point. Examples hereof are the US Maritime Strategy (and associated NATO naval strategies)[10], as well as the AirLand Battle[11] and FOFA doctrines[12]. On the other hand, the hitherto prevailing near-consensus on strategy seems to be unravelling, as may be gathered from the

No-First-Use[13] and NOD debates, and the growing support for these notions both in the public at large and amongst potential future governing parties (Labour Party, SPD, and others)[14].

7. *Naval forces, as well as other interventionary potentials, may remain outside the framework of arms control negotiations.* The two most powerful Western navies (those of the US and the UK) remain hostile to the notion of naval arms control, and even reject (cautious and modest) proposals for maritime C(S)BMs[15]. Since "it takes two (or in this case: three) to tango", the repeated Soviet initiatives in this direction (such as made e.g. in the Murmansk Speech by Gorbachev) may well come to nought, regardless of any political support they may receive from lesser NATO states, or from oppositional groupings in the major Western naval powers.

Political Trends

1. *The present blocs may, for all practical purposes, disintegrate, leaving all states at liberty to realign.* The Warsaw Pact has already been dissolved and NATO seems to be in dire straits as well, partly because of the disappearance of "the Enemy". Profound WEST-WEST disagreements exist in a wide range of problem areas, and to an increasing degree West European and American attitudes are set clearly apart (with the UK standing, in many respects, in an intermediary position).

EAST-EAST relations were even more crisis-ridden, even prior to the 1989 revolutions. The Soviet "thaw" associated with glasnost and perestroika was thus predestined to have repercussions in Eastern Europe, not merely in the shape of attempts at economic reform and effectivization, but also of demands for enhanced civil liberties and other human rights, including genuine national self-determination. As a consequence, the USSR was predestined to lose control over the satellite states sooner or later. The only way of preventing such an emancipation would have been by employment of brute military force, a solution which would, however, inevitably have jeopardized detente and thus hampered the West-to-East technology transfer which seems to be a precondition for preventing a collapse of perestroika. The USSR therefore had no alternative but to accept withdrawal from Eastern Europe and the complete dissolution of its alliance system, both unilaterally, economically and politically.

2. *The upsurge of nationalism may continue and intensify, perhaps to the point when claims for a revision of the "Yalta Map of Europe" may be raised by various states and/or groups within states.* The disintegration of the former Eastern bloc has already resulted in an upsurge of national strife and turmoil in and between East European countries, reflecting the fact that both the Eastern alliance and some East European states were in most respects artefacts, rather than "organic" state structures and alliances. The present national liberation struggles in the USSR, as well as the severe Hungarian-Romanian conflict (on both the state and intra-state level), are merely a few amongst a host of latent disputes that may well burst out into the open in the years to come[16]. Furthermore, the blossoming German nationalist sentiments testify to the fact that this is not an exclusively East European phenomenon. We have already seen indications that the struggles for national emancipation and self-determination may occasionally take on utterly unattractive forms and be accompanied by ethnocentrism, racism and violence. The spectacle of ethnic Hungarians being beaten to death with clubs by raving crowds of Romanians is far from a pretty one. Nor do shouts of "Ein Reich, Ein Volk" (heard in Leipzig) have a comforting sound, because they bring to mind (perhaps wrongly) the "missing" words "Ein Führer". [This section was written before the outbreak of civil war in Yugoslavia.]

3. *Germany may develop into an economic, political and military "Regional Superpower."* Subsequent to unification, Germany has become a power of such a standing economically and politically that it seems unlikely that it will acquiesce forever in any seeming discrimination in terms of its military potential.

4. *The USSR has effectively disintegrated into its constituent parts, roughly contiguous with the former union republics, henceforth sovereign states.* The USSR has been the last remaining great empire, and as such an obvious anachronism; just as the French and British colonial empires had to dissolve, so too did the Russian empire. The upsurge of nationalist sentiments has generated a pressure for complete political emancipation, though economic integration may remain.

5. *The US may "contract" by disengaging almost entirely from Europe, whilst maintaining far-flung global interests and a substantial interventionary potential to protect them.* Historically, all major empires have evolved through cycles of expansion and contraction, the latter most often preceded by (sometimes protracted) periods of increasingly costly and counterproductive over-extension, during which the discrepancy between the marginal costs of and the marginal gains accruing from foreign presence has continued to grow[17]. The US may well be in the middle of this intermediary stage and hence on the verge of contraction. A partial or complete withdrawal and disengagement from Europe would seem to be the obvious response, and would also be in conformity with the new geopolitical and economic realities, according to which the importance for the US of Japan and the NICs of the Pacific area is close to surpassing that of Europe.

However, by virtue of their economic potential, combined with a privileged insular position, the US will remain in a position to intervene abroad on a fairly large scale. This potential is, furthermore, a precondition for continuing to play the role of a genuine "superpower", and may be necessitated by the continued global interests of the US.

6. *The west European states, perhaps including certain former WTO/CMEA member states such as Hungary, may accomplish a "quantum leap" in integration, thus establishing a European Union, including a modicum of defence cooperation.* The European Community's 1992 goals may well prove a success, also because of the prevailing sense of urgency that springs from German unity and European "turbulence". Furthermore, the EC is working as a "magnet" on its surroundings, excerting an economic and political pull that may well attract both the NATO members presently remaining outside the EC (such as Norway), and neutrals (Austria and perhaps soon Sweden and Finland), as well as even former WTO/CMEA members. Whereas until recently only Hungary had spoken *expressis verbis* about these prospects, one could easily imagine both Czechoslovakia and Poland to be thinking along the same lines.

Dangers: The Nineties According to Murphy

From the above trends a number of dangers may arise. However, there are fortunately also mitigating factors, thanks to which the worst case predictions may not materialize. As a matter of fact, the present author does not believe they will, but only assumes the validity of "Murphy's Law" ("Everything that can go wrong will, at the worst possible moment") for the sake of the argument.

Military Hazards

1. *The "nuclear spectre" may be effectively removed, thus making war appear, once again, as a genuine political option for the external relations of states. Europe may thus become "safe for a conventional war."*

Argument: Although its validity is impossible to verify empirically, the assumption that nuclear weapons deter war would seem to possess a certain inherent plausibility. The fact that nuclear weapons of immense destructive power are available (and usable) implies that the prospects of war become highly unattractive, since the immense (indeed, most likely infinite) costs of nuclear war would invariably outweigh any prospective gains. As a consequence, wars that might otherwise have been fought may have been avoided.

Mitigating factors: Nuclear weapons cannot be "disinvented", and even subsequent to a hypothetical complete abolition, their "shadow" will remain: No party to a conflict will ever be in a position to feel entirely sure that its respective adversary may not have concealed some warheads, or may not clandestinely build some. In this sense, "existential deterrence" is an enduring feature of the post-1946 world, which will never entirely disappear[18].

2. *The world may experience a surge of nuclear proliferation.*

Argument: The NPT regime has been fragile all along[19], partly because it is so manifestly unjust and inequitable: The "haves" have simply dictated the terms to the "have-nots", and the latter understandably resent this. Until recently, however, the benefits that might seem to accrue from joining the exclusive "nuclear club" have been marginal, for two interconnected reasons: The superpowers were really "super", to the extent that no newcomer had any hopes of entering their "league". The best they might hope for was to become yet another "second-rate" nuclear power, in league with the UK and France. Secondly, bipolarity reigned, so that nuclear power could not be exerted by anybody, anywhere, or in any form, without triggering "central deterrence", i.e. the superpower arsenals, an outcome that would render the "independent" nuclear power redundant if not downright dangerous.

However, if the US and Soviet arsenals are built down considerably, whilst the British and French arsenals continue their expansion, the gap between the "first and second leagues" may no longer seem unbridgeable, and we may end up with a nuclear club consisting of four (or five, depending on how China is counted[20]) "full members", something that might raise the obvious question: "Why not six, seven, or even more?" The dissolution of the USSR has already been tantamount to an indirect proliferation, since one nuclear power has suddenly become four smaller nuclear (near-sovereign) states.

Mitigating factors: Nuclear weapons are not really all that useful. By means of them, a state can, of course, obliterate the civilian values of other states. It cannot, however, use nuclear arms for winning wars without causing such obliteration. Nuclear weapons are hence rather unsuitable for wars of conquest (unless one yearns for vast tracts of contaminated and uninhabitable ruins). Furthermore, the nuclear build-down on part of the present superpowers would be far from irreversible and the prospect of provoking a superpower rearmament (perhaps even with the two present superpowers acting in unison to stop or punish a perpetrator) might not be attractive at all to any would-be newcomer.

3. *Crisis instability may grow, hence increasing the risk of inadvertent (nuclear as well as conventional) war.*

Argument: This danger looms in both the conventional and the nuclear field, albeit for somewhat different reasons: In the nuclear field, crisis stability is constantly endangered by the increasing precision (and hence hard-target-kill capability) of strategic weapons. Unless steps are taken to "de-MIRV" strategic missiles, the risk that one side might acquire an actual disarming first strike capability may grow in parallel with the strategic nuclear build-down. It is simply easier to "take out" a hundred enemy ICBMs than a thousand or more, especially if a certain BMD potential is available (to guard against a few "misses"). The recent "Bush Initiative" seems to indicate a willingness to negotiate democracy of strategic missiles, but this may well be a very long-term perspective.

In the conventional field, quite substantial numerical reductions combined with a re-emphasis on offensive operational conceptions and an abandonment of forward defence as the guideline might lead to a situation in which comparatively small-scale, but highly mobile, armed forces come to be poised against each other along some new "Central Front". Each of these forces might hope to accomplish a swift and decisive victory by means of bold strikes. Under such conditions, "reciprocal fears of surprise attack"[21] might conceivably arise, and a pre-emptive conventional war might erupt as a result.

Mitigating factors: In the nuclear field, crisis stability is improving by virtue of the gradual substitution of mobile for fixed, silo-based ICBMs, as well as of the increasing range of SLBMs. In the conventional field, the dangers entailed by reductions are considerably mitigated by the emphasis placed in the CFE Treaty on offensive-capable weapons systems, combined with the lack of constraints on strictly defensive types of forces (e.g. barriers).

4. *"Forward defence" may be abandoned as the guideline for NATO and replaced with offensive manoeuvre warfare.*

Argument: It is hard to envisage a maintenance of the principle of forward defence by NATO, for two reasons. First of all, the notion of "forward" has become almost meaningless in the light of German unification. The former forward line would end up in the middle of Germany, and thus no longer be forward in any meaningful sense. A forward re-location to the new eastern border of Germany would be very costly, and undoubtedly quite unacceptable to both Poland and the USSR. Secondly, if the continuing CFE negotiations are going to accomplish further deep cuts in the conventional forces in Europe there simply will not be enough divisions to go around. The obvious alternative solution may come to be seen in some kind of offensive manoeuvre warfare, based on rather small, but highly mobile and lethal units in the style of the *AirLand Battle 2000*.

Mitigating factors: There are other alternatives to forward defence available, above all strictly non-offensive forms of indepth defence "*Raumverteidigung*" or "Territorial defence")[22]. These may well be selected.

5. *To the extent that the military situation in Europe is stabilized, European powers (including the two superpowers) may come to feel more at liberty to wage war elsewhere.*

Argument: The logic behind this danger is the so-called "stability/instability paradox"[23]: The more unstable a situation is perceived to be, the more caution and circumspection will the parties exercise, out of fear that events might otherwise escape control. In this sense an unstable situation may be remarkably stable.

The superpowers have scrupulously avoided any direct confrontation between American and Soviet forces, even in the remotest areas in the Third World. Conversely, if the underlying instability were to be removed, all parties involved might feel themselves liberated from former constraints. We might thus, once again, end up with direct US/Soviet *tête-a-tête* confrontations, from which might conceivably spring escalatory dynamics beyond control. At the very least, we might see unilateral interventions by European powers with imperial aspirations (Britain, France, Germany, Italy . . .?), prospects which may not seem at all attractive to Third World nations.

Mitigating factors: The "nuclear spectre" will continue to loom large in the minds of all states, not least the present superpowers, and the lessons already learned may not be all that easily forgotten. Some restraint would thus seem likely to endure, also because of the recent experience by both superpowers (Vietnam, Afghanistan) of the exorbitant costs and futility of intervention and anti-guerrilla warfare, which (according to the famous Lawrence of Arabia) is likely to be "messy and slow, like eating soup with a knife"[24]. Furthermore, to the extent that the East-West conflict is deprived of its present saliency, the likelihood of the two superpowers ending up on opposite sides in the same regional conflict will most likely decrease, as will its escalatory potential. [Since this was written, a US-led coalition intervened in Iraq to force its withdrawal from Kuwait, with the Soviet Union acquiescing.]

Political Hazards

1. *Europe may regress to the combined balance-of-power and war system of previous centuries.*

   Argument: As the present bipolar division of the world "withers away", it will become far from obvious that, say, (the welfare state capitalism of Scandinavian-type countries) has more in common with the more "austere" versions of capitalism (such as practised in, say, the UK of Mrs. Thatcher, or the US of Ronald Reagan or George Bush) than with "market socialism" (with "a human face") such as might be practised by Czechoslovakia or Hungary. Nor is it at all obvious that Turkey is a natural ally of Greece, Romania of Hungary, or Germany of France. If, in addition to this, nuclear deterrence is lifted as far as minor states and regional or local disputes are concerned (either because superpower deterrence loses all its credibility, or because the two superpowers cease to bother about minor allies), then small-scale wars between individual countries might re-emerge on the stage of intra-European relations.

   Mitigating factors: Europe may, on the other hand, have learned a lesson from the two world wars and their successor, the Cold War. They may have come to regard their own military force as having no legitimate use, except that of preventing others from using theirs.

2. *The world may revert to a modified bipolar system, with the USSR (or Russian and the other successor states) now contracting and reverting to a "Cold War" posture.*

Argument: The democratic development in the USSR may not be entirely irreversible: President Gorbachev may be ousted (as was Khrushchev in 1964), perhaps because of a blatant fiasco with perestroika, or he may die; subsequent to which a struggle for succession might erupt within the ruling elite(s) and other political (including the military). Old-style hardliners might conceivably prevail in this struggle, and see no alternative to a renewed cold war with the West. Although the East European alliance would undoubtedly be impossible to reforge, and even though the USSR may disintegrate, Russia would remain a great power, capable of generating military force of impressive proportions. Thanks to its relatively sheltered position, by virtue of the inaccessibility of the Russian "heartland" (cf. the failures of Napoleon and Hitler), as well as the residual nuclear deterrence, a disproportionate part of this military might go into offensive-capable forces that might well constitute a threat to neighbouring countries. [This was written before President Gorbachev's resignation.]

Mitigating factors: Societal processes are only rarely reversible: When history occasionally seems to repeat itself, it always does so "with a twist"[25]. Stalinism cannot therefore make a comeback, at least not in its old shape, since powerful democratic forces have been set free that would do their utmost to prevent this, as well as because the enhanced transparency of Soviet society would make it extremely difficult for any conspiracy to prevail. [This was written before the failed coup in the fall of 1991.]

Military Recommendations

In order to prevent the worst case from materializing, something has to be done about the dangers apparently inherent in the seemingly benign trends described above. There are, in principle, two approaches to thus enhancing security, which are far from mutually exclusive: the unilateral and the bilateral (informally coordinated or formally negotiated) approach.

A. *Bilateral measures*

As far as nuclear forces are concerned, the risks of low crisis stability and a surge of proliferation might be mitigated by taking the following precautions:

1. Establish a genuine "minimum deterrence regime";

2. Abandon the SDI programme, and scrap the Soviet ABM system;

3. Abandon plans for strategic anti-submarine warfare (i.e. at least one element in the Maritime Strategy of the US Navy), and prohibit (as a *quid pro quo*) forward deployment of Soviet SSBNs near the opponent's shores, as well as tests of depressed-trajectory SSBNs[26];

4. Set ceilings for British and French nuclear weapons well below the minimum deterrence level (say, at 100 warheads each);

5. Make all nuclear powers declare (as solemnly and bindingly as possible) a commitment to no-first-use of nuclear weapons;

6. Establish nuclear weapons-free zones, wherever possible (e.g. in the Nordic region and the Balkans);

7. Abolish (as a corollary of the no-first-use declarations) the entire range of battlefield and short-range nuclear weapons.

As far as conventional forces are concerned, the dangers of small-scale warfare and a resurgence of offensive manoeuvre warfare might be met by the following precautions:

1. Proceed, immediately, in the framework of the CFE (but revised in a non-bloc format), with negotiations on deep cuts (say, 50 percent or more of the remaining forces) in the same

categories of weaponry (tanks, armoured personnel carriers, artillery, helicopters, combat aircraft);

2. Establish a genuine "open skies regime" for the entire European area, as well as the US;

3. Proceed with negotiations on restrictive CSBMs with regard to ground and air forces, with a view to preventing provocative peacetime military activities;

4. Initiate immediate negotiations on maritime CSBMs (transparency-enhancing measures), copied directly from the Stockholm final document[27];

5. Launch preparatory negotiations on restrictive maritime CSBMs, such as exclusion zones, numerical and qualitative ceilings on exercises, geographical restrictions (e.g. no naval exercises within 100 nautical miles from the coast of other states without the consent of the latter);

6. Launch negotiations on "structural" naval arms control with a view to deep cuts in the realms of (especially nuclear-powered) attack submarines and major surface combatants (with a special view to abolishing aircraft carriers), as well as to complete abolition of tactical naval nuclear weapons[28].

In the realms of doctrines and weapons procurement, the following precautions might recommend themselves:

1. Conduct regular exchanges of views between high-ranking military professionals on questions of doctrine and other strategic conceptions. These should aim at identifying which elements of one side's strategic conceptions and posture are perceived as most threatening and provocative by the other side[29];

2. Take the first steps in the direction of preventative arms control by exchanging plans (say, under the auspices of the UN, or in some CSCE forum) for military R&D at an early stage (i.e. before major funding is decided upon by the

respective parliaments), and by giving the other side a formal right to be consulted.

As far as relations with the Third World are concerned, the following precautions might allay fears of a re-emergence of interventionism:

1. Establish formally (as solemnly and bindingly as possible) a non-intervention regime, which should curb the escalatory logic, according to which one side's arms sales are presently understood as legitimizing the other side's covert operations, which in their turn may warrant direct military involvement by the first party, etc. [30];

2. Initiate a new round of talks with a special view to curbing the proliferation of the most destabilizing (i.e. offensive-capable) types of weaponry[31];

3. Establish UN peace-keeping forces for naval purposes, and strengthen the existing arrangements for peace-keeping operations;

4. Specify a narrow range of circumstances under which direct military intervention by UN forces could occur (say, in order to prevent genocide), as well as the modalities of such intervention;

5. Seek a multilateral agreement obliging states to allocate a specified amount of their military savings (to be computed by an independent group of experts on the basis of an agreed data base) to development aid, to be channeled through the UN system.

B. Unilateral measures

As far as nuclear weapons are concerned, the following measures would seem relevant:

1. Define austere standards of sufficiency for assured destruction and reject all proposals for exceeding this limit as unwarranted and dysfunctional;

2. Abandon counterforce targeting;

3. Emphasize survivability in the development of new weapons. e.g. through preferring SLBMs to ICBMs, mobile to fixed installations, rearward to forward deployment, etc.

As far as conventional forces are concerned, the following measures would seem relevant:

1. Specialize, as far as possible, on strictly defensive types of military operations, e.g. by adapting to your home terrain;

2. Abandon all plans for deep strikes (deep interdiction) onto the adversary's territory. Scrap the weapons that are only suitable for this type of mission, and reconfigure 'dual-capable' weapons systems accordingly (from fighter-bombers to interceptors, and the like);

3. Combine maximum mobility on your own territory with minimum mobility beyond it, preferably in a "spider and web" mode[32];

4. Substitute, to the greatest possible extent, reserve forces for standing forces; short-range for long-range weapons; simple for complex weapon systems; dispersed teams for concentrated formations, etc.;

5. Specialize the air force for the following missions: establishment and maintenance of air superiority in your own airspace; short-range ground support; reconnaissance; and active air defence (i.e. interception of enemy aircraft)[33];

6. Substitute, as far as possible, SAMs for interceptors; helicopters (and VTOL planes) for fixed-wing aircraft; and RPVs for manned aircraft; take-off speed and hovering capacity for range, etc.;

7. Specialize the naval forces for the two missions of coastal defence against seawards invasion and the protection of vital sea lines of communication[34];

8. Substitute, as far as possible, land-based for sea-based weapons platforms; small surface combatants for large ones;

shore-based maritime airpower for carrier-based; anti-ship missiles for guns; stationary, yet 'stealthy', means of naval combat (sea mines and the like) for mobile ones; sub-surface to surface forces; etc.

As far as relations with the Third World are concerned, the following measures would seem relevant:

1. Abandon the last remnants of colonialism and imperialism such as (in the case of the UK) the Falkland Islands/Malvinas and (in the case of the RSFSR) most of the non-Russian union republics;

2. Abandon arms sales and especially sales of offensive-capable weapons to countries in volatile regions in the Third World, regardless of whether they have been motivated by commercial considerations, or by hopes of gaining political leverage[35];

3. Abandon other forms of military assistance, such as intelligence services and covert operations, to the Third World, especially in support of dictatorial regimes, be they of a conservative or a communist persuasion.

Conclusion

To conclude the paper on a holistic note, we end where we began: by returning once again to our "spiritual guide' through the yet unexplored wilderness of the nineteen-nineties, Heraclitus of Ephesus, who also has something to say about interdependence, global problems, and common security:

"Out of all things comes a unity,
and out of a unity all things."

"Listening not to me but to the Logos,
it is wise to agree that all things are one."

Notes

1. Quoted in Plato: *Kratylos*, p. 402A in the Stephanos pagination.

2. On the START negotiations, see e.g. Carter, April: *Success and Failure in Arms Control Negotiations*, (Oxford: Oxford University Press/SIPRI, 1989), pp. 183-200; Talbott, Strobe: *Deadly Gambits. The Reagan Administration and the Stalemate in Nuclear Arms Control*, (London: Pan Books, 1985), pp. 209-342; May, Michael, George F. Bing & John D. Steinbruner: *Strategic Arsenals After START: The Implications of Deep Cuts*, International Security, vol. 13, no. 1 (summer 1988), pp. 90-133; *Deep Cuts and Strategic Targeting. A Clarification*, ibid. vol. 14, no. 3 (winter 1989-90), pp. 194-197; Mendelsohn, Jack: START *Deals Cut at Jackson Hole*, Bulletin of the Atomic Scientists, vol. 45, no. 10, December 1989, pp. 25-28.

3. Cf. Kolodziej, Edward A.: *Modernization of British and French Nuclear Forces: Arms Control and Security Dimensions*, in Jacobsen, Carl G., ed.: *The Uncertain Course. New Weapons, Strategies, and Mindsets*, (Oxford: Oxford University Press/SIPRI, 1987), pp. 239-253; *British-French Nuclearization and European Denuclearization: Implications for USA Policy*, in Le Prestre, Philippe G., ed.: *French Security Policy in a Disarming World. Domestic Challenges and International Constraints*. (Boulder & London: Lynne Rienner Publishers, 1989), pp. 105-146.

4. Jervis, Robert: *The Meaning of the Nuclear Revolution. Statecraft and the Prospects of Armageddon*. (Ithaca: Cornell University Press, 1989), pp. 74-106; Cimbala, Stephen J.: *NATO Strategies and Nuclear Weapons* (London: Pinter Publishers, 1989), pp. 72-95.

5. Senghaas, Dieter: *Rüstung und Militarismus* (Frankfurt A.M.: Suhrkamp Verlag, 1972); Greenwood, Ted: *Making the MIRV: A Study in Defence Decision Making* (Cambridge, Mass.: Ballinger, 1975); Allison, Graham, T.: *What Fuels the Arms Race?*, in Reichart, John F. & Steven R. Sturm, eds.: *American Defence Policy*, Fifth Edition (Baltimore, Maryland: John Hopkins University Press, 1983), pp. 463-480; Allison, Graham T. & Morris, Frederic A.: *Armaments and Arms Control: Exploring the Determinants of Military Weapons*, Daedalus, Summer 1975, pp. 99-129; Albrecht, Ulrich: *The Role of Military R & D in Arms Build-Ups*, in Gleditsch, Nils Petter & Olav Njølstad, eds.: *Arms Races. Technological and Political Dynamics* (London: Sage, 1990), pp. 87-104; Thee, Marek: *Science-Based Military Technology as a Driving Force Behind the Arms Race*, ibid. pp. 105-120.

6. Cf. Robinson, Julian Perry: *Quasinuclear Weapons*, in Gutteridge, William & Trevor Taylor, eds.: *The Danger of New Weapons Systems* (London: Macmillan, 1983), pp. 151-165.

7. Cf. Barnaby, Frank: *The Automated Battlefield*, (New York: the Free Press, 1986).

8. For comprehensive surveys of Soviet and Eastern statements, see Holden, Gerald: *The WTO and Soviet Security Policy* (Oxford: Basil Blackwell, 1989), pp. 101-114; Garthoff, Raymond L.: *Gorbachev and Soviet Military Power*, The Washington Quarterly, vol. 11, no. 3, Summer 1988, pp. 131-158; McGwire, Michael: *New Directions in Soviet Arms-Control Policy, ibid.*, pp. 185-200; cf. Krause, Joachim: *Prospects for Conventional Arms Control in Europe*, Occasional Paper Series, no. 8 (New York: Institute for East-West Security Studies, 1988). On Non-offensive Defence, see e.g. my *Common Security and Non-Offensive Defense. A Neorealist Perspective* (Boulder, Col.: Lynne Rienner 1992); or my forthcoming *Alternative Defence Dictionary* (London: Adamantine Press, 1992).

9. Unterseher, Lutz: . . . *Der Ost macht ernst. Über die militärische und politische Bedeutung einseitiger Truppenreduzierungen der UdSSR und ihrer Verbündeten*, S + F. Vierteljahresschrift für Sicherheit und Frieden, vol. 7, no. 4, 1989, pp. 248-251.

10. Watkins, James D.: *The Maritime Strategy*, USA Naval Institute Proceedings, January 1986, pp. 2-17; Freidman, Norman: *The USA Maritime Strategy* (London: Jane's 1988); Brooks, Linton, F.: *Naval Power and National Security. The Case for the Maritime Strategy*, in Miller, Steven E. & Stephen van Evera, eds.: *Naval Strategy and National Security. An International Security Reader*, Princeton, N.J.: Princeton University Press, 1988, pp. 16-46. For a critique see e.g. Mearsheimer, John J.: *A Strategic Misstep: The Maritime Strategy and Deterrence in Europe, ibid.* pp. 47-101; or my own: *Crisis Stability and Non-Offensive Defence. A Nordic Perspective*, in Chalmers, Malcolm, Bjørn Møller - & David Stevenson: *Alternative Conventional Defense Structures for Europe. British and Danish Perspectives* (Mosbach: AFES-PRESS, 1989), pp. 1-65.

11. Headquarters, Department of the Army: *Field Manual 100-5: Operations*, (Washington, D.C.: Government Printing Office, 1982); cf. Richardson, William R.: *FM 100-5. The AirLand Battle in 1986*, Military Review, vol. 66, no. 3, 1986, pp. 4-11, cf. Kipp, Jacob W.: *Conventional Force Modernization and the Asymmetries of Military Doctrine: Historical Reflections on Air/Land Battle and the*

Operational Manoeuvre Group, in Jacobsen, ed. 1987: op. cit. (note 3), pp. 137-166.

12. Rogers, Bernard: *Sword and Shield: ACE Attack of Warsaw Pact Follow-On Forces*, NATO's Sixteen Nations, vol. 28, no. 1, January 1983, pp. 16-26; Farndale, Martin: *Follow-On Forces Attack, ibid.* vol. 3, no. 2, April/May 1988, pp. 42-50; Sutton, Boyd D., John R. Landry, Malcolm B. Armstrong, Howell M. Esles III & Wesley K. Clark: *Deep Attack Concepts and the Defence of Central Europe*, Survival, vol. 26, no. 2, 1984, pp. 50-78; Office of Technology Assessment: *New Technology for NATO. Implementing Follow-On Forces Attack*, (Washington, D.C.: Congress of the United States, 1987); Wijk, Rob de: *Deep Strike*, in Barnaby, Frank & Maries ter Borg, eds.: *Emerging Technologies and Military Doctrine. A Political Assessment*, (London: Macmillan, 1986) pp. 73-88.

13. See e.g. Bundy, McGeorge, George F. Kennan, Robert S. McNamara & Gerard Smith: *Nuclear Weapons and the Atlantic Alliance* (Foreign Affairs, Spring 1982), in Bundy, William P. ed.: *The Nuclear Controversy. A Foreign Affairs Reader*, (New York: New American Library, 1985), pp. 23-40; Union of Concerned Scientists: *No-First-Use*, (Washington, D.C.: UCS, 1983); Steinbruner, John D. & Leon V. Sigal, eds.: *Alliance Security: NATO and the No-First-Use Question*, (Washington, D.C.: The Brookings Institution, 1983); Blackaby, Frank, Josef Goldblatt & Sverre Lodgaard, eds.: *No-First-Use*, (London: SIPRI/Taylor & Francis, 1984); Lee, John Marshall: *No First Use of Nuclear Weapons*, in Hopmann P. Terrence & Frank Barnaby, eds.: *Rethinking the Nuclear Weapons Dilemma in Europe* (New York: St. Martin's Books), pp. 73-85.

14. See e.g. SPD: *Leitantrag Friedens- und Sicherheitspolitik in der vom Bundesparteitag der SPD in Nürnberg am 27. August 1986 beschlossenen Fassung*, Blätter für Deutsche und Internationale Politik, no. 10, 1986, pp. 1268-1278; *Frieden und Abrüstung in Europa. Beschluss zur Friedens- und Abrüstungspolitik des SPD-Bundesparteitages in Münster 30.8--2.9 1988*, Politik. Informationsdienst der SPD, 10 September 1988; Labour Party: *Defence and Security for Britain. Statement at the Annual Conference, 1984 by the National Executive Committee*, (Manchester: Labour Party, 1984); Gapes, Mike: *Labour's Defence and Security Policy*, in Hopmann & Barnaby, eds.: op. cit. (note 13), pp. 341-355.

15. Cf. Haesken, Ole & al.: *Confidence Building Measures at Sea*, FFI/Rapport, no. 88/5002 (Kjeller, Norway: Forsvarets Forskningsinstitut, 1988); Wiberg, Hökan: *Maritime tillidsskabende foranstaltninger*, Working Papers, no. 3 (Copenhagen: Centre for

Peace and Conflict Research, 1990); Shasholsky, Nikolai: *The Problem of Limiting and Reducing Naval Activities and Naval Armaments*, in IMEMO: *Disarmament and Security. Yearbook 1988-1989*, (Moscow: Novosti, 1989), pp. 337-340. For a critical assessment, see Hill, J.R.: *Arms Control at Sea* (London: Routledge, 1989), pp. 1985-201; *Superpower Naval Arms Control: Practical Considerations and Possibilities*, in Fieldhouse, Richard, ed.: *Security at Sea. Naval Forces and Arms Control*, (Oxford: Oxford University Press/SIPRI, 1990), pp. 118-134.

16. Brzezinski, Zbigniew: *Post-Communist Nationalism, Foreign Affairs*, vol. 68, no. 5, Winter 1989/90, pp. 1-25.

17. Kennedy, Paul: *The Rise and Fall of the Great Powers. Economic Change and Conflict from 1500 to 2000*, (London: Unwin Hymann Ltd., 1988), especially the chapter on the USA facing decline, pp. 514-535. Cf. Gilpin, Robert G.: *War and Change in World Politics*, (Cambridge: Cambridge University Press, 1981), pp. 186-210.

18. Cf. Bundy, McGeorge: *Existential Deterrence and its Consequences*, in Maclean, Douglas, ed.: *The Security Gamble*, (Totowa, N.J.: Rowman & Allanhead, 1986), pp. 3-13.

19. On the background and limitations of the NPT, see e.g. Myrdal, Alva: *The Game of Disarmament. How the United States and Russia Run the Arms Race* (New York, 1976: Pantheon Books), pp. 159-193. On the present risks of proliferation, see e.g. Spector, Leonard, S.: *Nuclear Proliferation Today* (New York, 1984: Vintage Books); Meyer, Stephen M.: The Dynamics of Nuclear Proliferation, (Chicago, 1984: The University of Chicago Press).

20. I completely omit from this analysis the two unquestionable, yet undeclared, nuclear states Israel and South Africa, which are not really comparable.

21. Cf. Schelling, Thomas: *The Strategy of Conflict*, (Cambridge, Mass., 1960: Harvard University Press), pp. 207-229.

22. Cf. my: *Resolving the Security Dilemma in Europe. The German Debate on Non-Offensive Defence*, (London: Brassey's Defence Publishers, 1991).

23. Cf. Jervis: op. cit. (note 4), pp. 19-22, 76-78; Snyder, Glenn: *The Balance of Power and the Balance of Terror*, in Seabury, Paul, ed.: *The Balance of Power*, (San Francisco: Chandler, 1965), pp. 184-201.

24. Cf. Gibson, James William: *The Perfect War. The War We Couldn't Lose and How We Did.* (New York, 1988: Vintage Books); Urban, Mark: *War in Afghanistan.* (New York: St. Martin's Press, 1988).

The quotation is from Lawrence, Thomas Edward: *The Seven Pillars of Wisdom. A Triumph*, (London: Jonathan Cape 30 Bedford Square, 1935), pp. 192-193.

25. Cf. Marx, Karl (paraphrasing an obscure passage from Hegel): *Der achzehnte Brumaire des Louis Napoleon* (1852), in - & Friedrich Engels: *Werke*, vol. 8 (Berlin: Dietz Verlag, 1975), p. 115.

26. The rationale for the latter is that these are potential means for 'decapitation' strikes against the US command structure (the NCA), and/or against the airbreathing 'leg' of the strategic 'triad'. See e.g. Carter, Ashton B.: *Assessing Command System Vulnerability*, in John D. Steinbruner & Charles A. Zraket, Eds.: *Managing Nuclear Operations*, (Washington, D.C.: The Brookings Institution, 1987), pp. 217-281; cf. Purver, Ronald G.: *Arms Control Proposals for the Arctic: A Survey and Critique*, in Mötöla, Kari, ed.: *The Arctic Challenge. Nordic and Canadian Approaches to Security and Cooperation in an Emerging International Region*, (Boulder, Westview Press, 1988) pp. 183-221, especially pp. 202-208.

27. Cf. Howard, Patrick: *Naval Confidence-Building Measures: a CSCE Perspective*, in Fieldhouse, ed.: op. cit. (note 15), pp. 226-237.

28. Cf. Fieldhouse, Richard: *Naval Nuclear Arms Control*, in - ed.: op. cit. (note 15), pp. 158-186; Lin, Herbert: *Verification of Nuclear Weapons at Sea, ibid.* pp. 102-117.

29. Cf. Hamm, Manfred R. & Hartmut Pohlman: *Military Strategy and Doctrine: Why They Matter to Conventional Arms Control*, The Washington Quarterly, vol. 13, no. 1, Winter 1990, pp. 185-198.

30. Cf. Forsberg, Randall: *The Case for a Third-World Non-intervention Regime*, (Brookline, Mass: IDDS, 1987: Manuscript).

31. Cf. Nolan, James E.: *The US.-Soviet Conventional Arms Transfer Negotiations*, in George, Alexander L., Philip, J. Farley & Alexander Dallin, eds.: *USA-Soviet Security Cooperation. Achievements, Failures, Lessons*, New York: Oxford University Press, pp. 510-523; Catrina, Christian: *Arms Transfers and Dependence*, (New York: Taylor & Francis/UNIDIR, 1988), pp. 129-132.

32. SAS (Studiengruppe Alternative Sicherheitspolitik), eds.: *Vertrauensbildende Verteidigung. Reform deutscher Sicherheitspolitik*, (Gerlingen: Bleicher Verlag, 1989), especially Unterseher, Lutz: *Bauprinzipien alternativer Landstreitkräfte*, (pp. 149-164).

33. For an elaboration on this and the subsequent point, see my: *Air Power and Non-Offensive Defence. A Preliminary Analysis*, Working Papers No. 2, (Copenhagen: Centre for Peace and Conflict Research, 1989).

See also Unterseher, Lutz: *Umrisse einer stabilen Luftverteidigung*, in SAS: op. cit (note 32), pp. 188-203.

34. For an elaboration on this and the subsequent point, see my *Restructuring the Naval Forces. Maritime Aspects of a Non-Offensive Defence*, in Borg, Marlies & Wim Smit, eds.: *Non-provocative Defence as a Principle of Arms Control*, (Amsterdam: Free University Press, 1989), pp. 189-206.

35. That arms sales do not provide the exporting country with significant leverage vis-á-vis the importing state is argued elaborately in Pierre, Andrew: *The Global Politics of Arms Sales*. (Princeton, N.J.: Princeton University Press, 1982).

Appendix A

Glossary of Acronyms

BMD	Ballistic Missile Defence
CFE	Conventional Forces in Europe
CMEA	Council for Mutual Economic Assistance (Eastern Europe)
CPSU	Communist Party of the Soviet Union
CSCE	Conference on Security and Cooperation in Europe
C(S)BMs	Confidence (and Security) Building Measures
EC	European Community
FOFA	Follow-On Forces Attack
ICBM	Inter-Continental Ballistic Missile
INF	Intermediate-range Nuclear Forces
MIRV	Multiple Independent Re-entry Vehicles
NATO	North Atlantic Treaty Organization
NICs	Newly Industrializing Countries
NOD	Non-Offensive Defence
NPT	Non-Proliferation Treaty
RP	Remotely Piloted Vehicle
RSFSR	Russian Soviet Federated Socialist Republic
R&D	Research and Development
SAM	Surface-to-Air Missile
SLBM	Sea-Launched Ballistic Missile
SPD	Social-Democratic Party of Germany
SSBNs	Strategic Submarine, Ballistic, Nuclear
START	Strategic Arms Reduction Talks
VTOL	Vertical Take Off and Landing
WTO	Warsaw Treaty Organization

Regional Security Associations: Application to Europe and Other Regions

ARNOLD SIMONI *

General Model for a Regional Security Association

The central element in the Regional Security Association approach is the negotiation of a comprehensive treaty of cooperation by the states within a region interested in creating a genuine, non-threatening security community, perhaps with broader political and economic purposes attached as well. The primary creation of an RSA Treaty would be a regionally-oriented, but essentially autonomous multilateral security force, that would largely or completely replace national military forces within the region. It would perform the functions of a defence force, border guard, a verification agency and also could incorporate other paramilitary functions such as environmental and resource monitoring. The emphasis and structure of the RSA's security force would depend upon the individual region and its unique concerns and character. There would be one principle, however, guiding the development of the security force which would apply to all regions: it must neither create, nor be perceived to create, a military vacuum within the region, nor be seen to have an aggressive

* The author would like to thank the members of the York University, Centre for International and Strategic Studies for their assistance in preparing this paper. In particular, the text has profited from several discussions with the Deputy Director Keith Krause, the Centre's Senior Research Associate, James Macintosh and Hanna Newcombe, Director of the Peace Research Institute-Dundas.

posture that could threaten or be perceived to threaten neighbours.

A Military-Policy-Security and Verification Force for RSA

Such a regional security force must not and cannot follow the model of NATO, the Warsaw Treaty Organization or similar defence arrangements. NATO was designed not only to defend itself, but also to retaliate and, if deemed necessary, to make a preemptive attack. The WTO also employed a vaguely similar, offensively configured posture and doctrine. The line between defence and offence is very thin and is made no more easy to distinguish by modern conventional weapons. By contrast, as indicated above, an RSA's security efforts would only be directed at developing non-threatening defence capabilities. A well-prepared defensive system, concentrating its efforts on modern anti-ship, anti-tank and anti-aircraft weapons and employing a well-disciplined and trained military force (including a Militia Force), would fulfil these needs. Such a military force would act as an effective deterrent dissuading possible outside aggressors. Moreover, open conflict between nations who have joined the RSA would be avoided, or at least kept under control, because the united RSA military force would enter into action in the event of any internal conflict. In addition, the nations directly involved in the RSA would be the only ones responsible for the implementation of agreements reached by the participating states. This would reduce or eliminate the chances of political interference by third parties.

This regional security force would also carry out police or border guard and — very important — compliance verification functions among the nations within the regional organization, in a manner agreed on by the participating states. Depending on the region's political stability, a militia or home guard could be an additional component in the overall security design, helping to underwrite the region's self-defence capabilities at a reasonable cost.

The verification function of the RSA's autonomous security force would serve two purposes. First, it would raise and maintain trust among the nations within a region by ensuring through its independent monitoring that all participating states were complying with the initial RSA Treaty's disarmament terms. Second, through this monitoring function, it would also ensure non-participating neighbours and more distant but interested states that none of the region's individual members possessed threatening offensive capabilities. It would ensure, as a consequence, that the region would not undertake any aggressive action against outside nations and thus would eliminate any pretext for being attacked as well. This verification function would serve and be complemented by an associated collection of transparency-enhancing confidence and security-building measures.

The characteristics of this defence-policy-verification force can be summarized in the following way: The force could be compared to the functioning of a national police force in the sense that its operations would have to remain within the legal framework established by the individual RSA. It would be expected to act automatically, in accordance with criteria established in the constitution of the regional grouping, and would not have to wait for a special mandate or collective political deliberation to perform its tasks. As far as the size, armament, and activities of the force are concerned, these would have to be well-defined in the founding Treaty.

The staff for the military-police force would be recruited from the forces of all participating nations, freely intermixing personnel. This staff would wear a distinctive uniform. Individuals would temporarily surrender their national status, and would work for the RSA only. The personnel would be located at strategically positioned bases, close to sensitive border regions, airports and other transportation centres.

The participating nations of the regional association would have to agree that all proscribed heavy military equipment be destroyed in an agreed manner, including (should there be any) chemical and nuclear weapons and their delivery vehicles. In addition, the movement of these types of equipment through any of the participant countries by non-regional powers would almost certainly have to be forbidden.

A review board and an ombudsman with distinctive power would have to be established to ensure the perception as well as the fact of fairness in the force's operation. In addition, it is important to emphasize that changes in an RSA's founding constitution could only be made with the participants' consent. Thus, nations would not have to be afraid of harmful or undesired changes in the constitution being made without their consent. The RSA's constitution would have to be worked out in all of its details before nations formally joined the organization. Nations wishing to leave the association would need to provide at least one year's notice of intent.

In addition to military security, the economy of a nation and the well-being of its people (including their human rights) are obviously major concerns, if for no other reason than the fact that political and military stability cannot be maintained if economic conditions within a nation, and in this case within a region, do not provide for the basic needs of the people. Depending on the region, close economic cooperation between the nations involved would be important. In many areas, such as Central America, Southern Africa and others, cooperation leading to the formation of a common market would be essential. This would certainly be the case – although a special case – in Europe, where extremely complex and dynamic integrative economic processes are already under way.

From this general model of a Regional Security Association, let us now turn to specific examples.

An RSA Adapted for Central Europe

The argument is often made that Europe, as a result of the participation of most European states in many different regional organizations such as the European Economic Community, will become an integrated community of nations, with no fear of war within the region. However, this assessment is plausible only as long as present expectations hold true about the growth of the European Common Market and the development of political stability within the larger group of 34 European CSCE (Conference on Security and Cooperation in Europe) member states.

The so-called "Two Plus Four" (FRG, GDR, USA, USSR, UK, France) agreement has very quickly led to a unified Germany. The political situation in Europe may change as a result of German unification. Having the largest population and being economically the strongest nation in Europe, Germany may change her political outlook and direction dramatically during the coming years. Internal political pressure for revision of its Eastern borders, and the "need" to reinforce its military forces against a real or perceived threat from the east, might make the new Germany a military power to be reckoned with.

We do not live in a static period and there is little reason to believe that the profound changes which have taken place during 1989-1990 in Eastern and Central Europe will be consolidated in a short period of time. Rather, the contrary can be expected. Eastern Europe will surely encounter grave political and economic problems. More to the point, the chances are slim that the Soviet Union, which is passing through a painful process of ethnic nationalism and separatism combined with profound economic problems, will have a liberal democratic government and a functioning economy in the next five to ten years. Rather, one can expect that the Soviet Union will be politically and economically unstable. Furthermore, ethnic and religious groups within the Soviet Union will exert increasing centrifugal pressures, adding to the already daunting array of problems facing the Soviet leadership. The Soviet Union, having lost the Warsaw Pact nations and confronted with so many serious problems, is bound to feel exposed and insecure. This will be the case particularly with the two Germanies having fused into one "Greater Germany". The Soviet Union could turn back to military solutions, diverting resources to its armed forces. It must not be forgotten, as well, that the Soviet Union, or Russia as its main successor, will remain a major nuclear power and a military superpower, whatever other changes may occur.

How would Germany react to this counter-productive, instinctive arming by the Soviet Union? Being a strong industrial country, it would have no difficulty in producing large quantities of modern weapons, including nuclear systems. The vicious circle of mistrust and the rationale that more weapons are needed for deterrence would start again. In an unstable and unpredictable environment, other powerful nations would react in the same way. We need only to remind ourselves that all industrial nations - as well as many that are not very advanced industrially - are producing and acquiring modern weapons and have used them in the recent past. Iraq is the best example of this trend.

It is therefore extremely important for the stability of Europe and in fact for the world, that the Soviet Union does not feel threatened by developments within neighbouring East and Central European countries and the growth of an increasingly powerful and independent Germany. An RSA would ensure that no nation in this region could acquire or buy armaments which could be used for aggressive purpose and/or without the knowledge of the other partners of the region. Thus, it can be hoped that the development of a non-threatening, but militarily credible, defence-oriented regional security association of states on the periphery of the Soviet Union does act both as a non-provocative buffer and barrier against military actions directed either way. The formation of regional associations in Central and Eastern Europe would provide a viable and non-threatening security structure throughout Europe.

An RSA in the Balkans

With the end of Soviet control in the Balkans, new positive developments in this traditionally difficult region are taking place. The historic meeting of the Prime Minister of Turkey, Mr. Turgut Ozal, with his Greek counterpart, Mr. Andreas Papandreou in Switzerland in January 1988 and the exploratory discussions to investigate the possibility of developing closer co-operation amongst Turkey, Greece, Rumania, Bulgaria, and Yugoslavia are very promising.

In the middle of October 1990, the foreign ministers of Albania, Bulgaria, Greece, Romania, Turkey and Yugoslavia met in Tirana, Albania. They agreed to pursue closer cooperation amongst themselves and undertook to protect minority rights. They also acknowledged the principles of respect for independence, sovereignty, territorial integrity, inviolability of frontiers, equal rights and non-interference in internal affairs. These aims, expressed by the foreign ministers of the nations, are certainly laudable, especially coming from a region where there are strong differences in political and ideological orientation and adversarial relations amongst several of the region's states.

The arguments developed in the previous section discussing the virtues of the RSA idea in the East and Central European context are generally valid in the Balkans as well. This is particularly so for the security association's value in reducing intra-regional conflict. It would play a very important role in this region.

The formation of a Regional Security Association in the Balkans would allow the states in this region to ensure that the sentiments expressed in Tirana could become reality. This would also allow them to concentrate their efforts on improving their economic conditions. [Since this was written, the civil war in Yugoslavia further showed the need for a stabilizing structure in the Balkan region.]

An RSA for the Baltic States

One of the most important reasons why the Soviet Union is con-cerned about the independence of the Baltic states is geostrategic. The perceived danger for the Soviet Union is that the waterway to Leningrad could be blocked. The offsetting reality, however, is that Lithuania, Latvia, and Estonia have acquired independence. One can assume that the Soviet Union might be reas-sured if the long-term effective neutrality of these states could be ensured. A non-threatening regional security community (probably encompassing Finland as well) could fulfil this aim. It may be the only feasible way to ensure that they remain on good terms with the Soviet Union. The RSA approach could very well satisfy the basic requirements of all relevant actors.

An RSA in the Middle East

The danger that a conflict in the Middle East could quickly grow out of control, engaging the superpowers and other interested major powers, is widely recognized. It is generally appreciated, as well, that this could lead to nuclear and/or chemical conflagration. The recent invasion of Kuwait by Iraq and the subsequent war against Iraq by the US-led coalition is a compelling illustration. It is also obvious that the latent conflict between Israel, the Palestinians, and the Arab countries has deep roots. One could hardly expect that diplomatic negotiation or agreements between the Palestinians and Israel could alone eliminate the conflict or bring about a peaceful relationship. Neither should one expect that time alone will somehow improve the situation. The opposite will more likely be the case. As time passes, political tension in the Gaza Strip and on the West Bank can only increase internal upheavals in the Israeli-occupied territories as well as create trouble for outside powers.

But even more important is the realization that the Persian Gulf is a vital supplier of oil around the world. Thus, any disruption of the oil supply not only hurts the shareholders of the large oil corporations but, in a real sense, would have serious consequences for most countries which are dependent upon this vital energy resource.

The ongoing militarization of the Middle East makes matters particularly dangerous. In addition to Israel's having 300 nuclear warheads, Pakistan and others hope to produce nuclear warheads in this decade. As we have seen, Iraq has attempted to build its own nuclear weapons; though this has been stopped, there is no doubt that other nations could do the same. It is imperative that we find solutions to this extremely important and complex regional problem. It would be naive to believe that everything will be fine if Saddam Hussein could only be eliminated.

An attempt to form an RSA in this region could start with Israel, Egypt, Jordan, Syria and Lebanon joining together. It could be an important beginning for reducing the tension in this region. Obviously, the Palestinian question would have to be solved and the attitude of Israel completely changed. The necessary

political changes which could lead Israel to consider such an association would be the realization that they cannot depend forever on the financial support by the United States, which is now under pressure to reduce its own expenditures for domestic political reasons.

The promise of extensive economic cooperation, whereby Israel could supply industrial goods to its neighbouring states, and the possibility of major reductions in current expenditures for the military sector, combined with reduced financial support from the US (especially for Israel and Egypt), would be important motivating factors for moving in this direction.

Conclusion

The existing global trend of "improvements" in the effectiveness of all weapons, and the ongoing proliferation of modernized conventional, nuclear, chemical and bacteriological weapons are facts of our time. Furthermore, the prospect that local conflicts can escalate is a very real danger. The global political-military systems have never been static in the past and certainly are not today.

The formation of Regional Security Associations, as proposed here, would help in reducing the risk that conflicts between small and medium-sized nations could escalate and eventually involve the nuclear powers. RSAs would be an

important contributing factor which could help to establish and maintain peace. They would serve the self-interest of all nations, both those directly involved and those outside of such regional associations. Their adoption could be the first step leading towards the reduction of international tensions and the danger of open confrontation.

Thus, the development of RSA-style security communities could become a very important step in the transition to a world without war. Their adoption could also help to address, in a stabilizing manner, difficult regional political and economic problems. Because contemporary political conditions are more than usually fluid, now is a particularly good time to take steps toward the development of RSAs. As time passes, the difficulties facing their implementation will grow.

Helsinki Treaty Federation

HANNA NEWCOMBE

As a Central European (born in Prague, Czechoslovakia in 1922) I have often felt somewhat uneasy with the claim of the European Community (EC) to be an incipient "European Federation". I would always want to insist that this was only a "West-European Federation" that was being born. I have even resented the term "Eastern Europe". Czechoslovakia has always considered itself to be part of Central Europe, which is not just a geographical term, but a claim to central importance in European history.

After the recent changes in Central Europe and the Balkans, the opportunity opens up to create a truly Pan-European Federation that would finally create a true "zone of perpetual peace" in this cultural heartland, the way the EC has done between France and Germany. But it is an opportunity that may escape us, because several competing rearrangements are trying to rush into the political vacuum.

One danger is that we may unwittingly recreate pre-World War II conditions by installing a strong unified Germany in the heart of Central Europe. Hitler may not have been a unique villain, but a product of the geopolitical forces generated by such a configuration – in which case the tragedy is possibly repeatable.

Another danger is that of unwittingly recreating the conditions prior to World War I, when "Balkans" meant instability, like today's Middle East, and a Serbian terrorist's bullet brought about a slowly accelerating accidental war that nobody wanted.

There is a variety of other scenarios that are not quite as horrendous, but nevertheless not as desirable as a fully federated Europe (East and West). For example: (1) Inviting the newly liberated states of Central and Eastern Europe to join EC, either en bloc or one by one: or doing the same with NATO. This arrangement would be Western-dominated rather than symmetrical, which might indeed reflect the real economic strength, but would nevertheless be of doubtful long-range sustainability. (2) A merger of NATO and WTO into a unified all-European security system. Although symmetrical along East-West lines, this would nevertheless leave out the European neutrals, and therefore not be really all-European.

Federation is usually conceived as a political arrangement between contiguous geographic units to unite some of their policy concerns under a common government. Or alternatively, a unitary state may devolve some of its functions to smaller constituent geographic units without dissolving or abandoning all its functions. Whether formed from below or from above, by partial fusion or partial fission, a federation ends up as a structure of subsidiarity – a two-level structure with divisions of responsibility more or less clearly defined. It might even be a multi-level "wedding cake" structure, if municipal and neighbourhood government is added at the lower end, and continental and global government at the upper end.

However, another parameter should be considered in thinking about possible new patterns in Europe. This additional parameter is the looseness or tightness (degree of integration) of the federal bond. Federalist thinkers have often made a dichotomy between a league or confederation on the one hand and a true federation on the other, the former being merely a treaty between governments, while the latter has a popularly elected legislative assembly for the federal unit. It remains a useful distinction; but this should not blind us to the possibility of inventing new intermediate forms if the situation seems to demand it.

It is always a problem in federations to negotiate an appropriate and well-defined division of functions and responsibilities. This has been a perennial problem in Canada, perhaps even more acutely than in most of the other 16 federal states in the world; but this problem is always present. It is sometimes formulated as obtaining a balance between centralization and decentralization; but sometimes it is more crucial to decide *which* powers will be exercised by each level than *how many* powers. If a federation is also a multinational state, as many of them are, the two lines of cleavage (federal-provincial and inter-ethnic) may reinforce each other and create considerable tension. This produces pressures toward inventing new forms, to prevent outright partition or separation.

One response has been "consociational democracy" as practiced e.g. in Belgium (which is not a federation) and Austria (a federation which has no ethnic division, but a religious one). Its features are: prearranged levels of government posts for each nationality or interest bloc; minority veto on certain decisions (since simple majority rule would be oppressive), a minimum national consensus (leaving controversial issues aside) and a considerable degree of sectoral autonomy. The ethnic or religious communities are not always geographically segregated, which makes a simple federal solution impossible. Consociational democracy is a compromise between individual rights, which demand simple majority decisions, and group rights, which require entrenchment of some minority rights. Forms of consociational democracy may ease ethnic tensions which might arise in a federated Europe.

Another structure which has arisen in the Canadian context is "sovereignty association". This has not yet been completely defined, but it seems to mean political independence of the units while maintaining complete economic integration. Movement toward it would be in the opposite direction to that being traversed by the EC, but arrive at the same end result. If it proves a useful solution for Quebec, it might be equally applicable to nascent semi-autonomous Soviet Republics. "Technology transfer" should include political as well as scientific inventions. It now seems that Soviet Republics will precede Quebec in making this change.

The main requirement is emotional detachment from state-splitting issues; even partition is not the end of the world. We should regard states (governments) merely as useful administrative services to citizens, not objects of idolatrous worship. Then we can negotiate rationally which form would serve citizens the best, not which super-creature must live or die.

However, in the European situation, we face another problem. There we have the system of nation-states, until recently tightly organized into two mutually hostile blocs, with a few neutrals outside the blocs. There is the prospect of a unified Germany in the middle of the continent, liable to become the strongest regional power, and with a historical record of starting two world wars in this century. Superimposed on this are several regional organizations, none of them quite a federation: e.g. NATO, WTO, EC, EFTA, Council of Europe, COMECON, CSCE.[1] How should this structure be rationalized in a post-Cold-War world?

Here I want to introduce the concept of "nested quasi-federations", a rather messy arrangement of a fairly compact (rather well integrated, economically at least) central cluster (EC with its impending extension in 1992), embedded in a much looser, but more comprehensive CSCE framework, also gradually integrating, eventually into a "Helsinki Federation" of 34 states (now 37 with the 3 Baltic Republics.) The Helsinki Federation would extend beyond Europe (East, West and neutral) into North America (US and Canada) and the USSR (including its Asian part), thus anchoring Europe (with its potential German instability) to the superpowers. It is worth noting that this huge CSCE territory extends through most of the Northern temperate zone of the Earth, the main exception being Japan and China.

However, another multinational grouping, the Organization for Economic Cooperation and Development (OECD) includes Japan, along with North America and Western Europe (the old "Trilateral" group of economic superpowers), and this might gradually federate as well, being already generally considered to be a zone of stable or permanent peace. Economic rivalries might interfere with this process, but perhaps could be overcome. China perhaps should be considered part of the South.

My point is that the overlapping CSCE and OECD regions (where economic leadership is provided by the Summit of Seven) would complete the Northern temperate belt and if both regions gradually federalize, the overlap might be reconcilable under flexible arrangements that we could invent. I have no details to offer as yet, but perhaps overlapping as well as nested quasi-federations could be accommodated as part of a cross-linked, gradually "jelling" comprehensive global order. In any case large-scale regional considerations such as the foregoing might be developed into a new geo-politics of peace.

The south (tropical belt) regions should not be left out, of course,. It is a great worry that they are not yet a zone of stable peace; parts of it (the so-called "fuse" from Southern Africa through the Middle East and South Asia to South East Asia) are instead a system of almost permanent war, and there weapons of all sorts are proliferating through trade, technology transfer, and local production. Their regional organizations are weak, though ASEAN is hopeful. But in this essay (though not in the real world) we must leave the South aside. "One problem at a time" must be the rule.

We just now consider the proposed nested structure of the new Europe in a little more detail. I propose that NATO and WTO, being military alliances, are no longer needed and should dissolve. WTO has announced the abandonment of its military functions and is politically broken up already.

The alternative proposal sometimes advocated for NATO is a change of function from military to political, and a widening to admit not only all of unified Germany, but also any East European countries who wish to join. I would consider such a revamped and widened NATO superfluous at best; and at worst, as a remnant of the Cold War, a symbol of "victory" of West over East accompanied by "absorption" of "conquered territories" by the "occupier" – all obsolete military concepts that would better be forgotten. We want to unify all of Europe on a basis of symmetrical equality, not asymmetric victory-defeat structures. Common security must not be imperialistic.

Symbolism does matter, and impulses toward revanchism might be ignited if we are not careful.

EC with its present membership should continue to proceed toward the projected 1992 target of complete economic integration, and beyond that, plan complete political integration on a federal basis in a not-too-distant future. It should not admit any new members at this time, since this would delay integration, as the new members would need time to catch up. For EC, deepening rather than widening should be the order of the day.

CSCE, on the other hand, is wide rather than deep; comprehensiveness is its main asset but the degree of integration is low. No new members need to be added (except Albania). CSCE is comprehensive already; but it is at the other pole from EC in coherence or degree of integration. The Helsinki Final Document of 1975 is not even a treaty, just the final document of the first conference, yet it has been functioning somewhat as a treaty, or at least an agreement. It has stabilized the post-WW II boundaries of Europe, thus acting as a surrogate for the non-existent peace treaty to end that war. It has also strongly addressed human rights concerns, as well as security issues and issues of economic cooperation, in its "three baskets".

Yet CSCE is usually described more as a process than as a structure; becoming, not being, in philosophical terms. The process has been transacted in a series of conferences, and has accelerated when CSCE accepted new responsibilities for conventional arms reduction negotiations in Europe (the Conventional Forces in Europe, CFE, negotiations), whose first stage was concluded in Autumn 1990. It already has to its credit the Stockholm Treaty on Security and Confidence-Building Measures of 1986. The "process" will finally yield a "structure", or several of them: perhaps one dealing with security (European Security Organization, ESO, as proposed by Malcolm Chalmers in World Policy Journal, Spring 1990), one with economics (building on the already existing UN Economic Commission for Europe, which includes all of Europe but not North America), one working on political integration and one formulating a common foreign policy. The CSCE Conference in Paris in the Fall of 1990 has already created some incipient structures.

It is clear that, for many years to come, CSCE would be much more loosely integrated than the EC, which would be nested completely within it like a hard nugget in a soft pudding. If arrangements are carefully worked out (problems must be foreseen, but hopefully solvable ones), the fact that Western European states would belong to two incipient federations simultaneously need not interfere with the integration process in either one. A formal link between EC and CSCE might be desirable, to iron out any difficulties. Nesting and overlapping of administrative units is probably a good idea for another reason. Dividing the Earth's surface by neat lines, so that the units contained within them cover the surface entirely and without overlaps, is an expression of territoriality, which in both humans and animals is linked to aggression. If that is so, then to mix it up a bit, make it more complex, should help to overcome that tragic flaw in human nature.

In the possible additional overlap with the Organization for Economic Cooperation and Development (OECD), Canada and US would also have a double membership (in CSCE and OECD) and Western European states triple membership. Even that additional complication could be accommodated, I believe, though it would take time to sort it out.

In conclusion, I will add a few comments about a suitable name and a capital for the incipient CSCE federation. Unpronounceable acronyms or long full names do not inspire sufficient pride or enthusiasm – we need better symbols that reverberate emotionally. Notwithstanding my earlier statement that governmental arrangements are just a matter of convenience, not allegiance, we need some attraction to carry us through the transition from old to new forms.

Helsinki Federation would not do, because I am about to propose a capital other than Helsinki. *Pan-Europe* is not suitable because it does not include North America or North and Central

Asia. I reach into geological theories of tectonic plates which move continents about. Before the Atlantic Ocean opened up through rifting about 80 million years ago, the Northern Continent was unified from the West Coast of North America to the East Coast of North Asia. That ancient supercontinent is now called *Laurasia* by geologists. I therefore propose that this supercontinent, from Vancouver to Vladivostok, with the double sign of "V for Victory", be named *Laurasia*, and become a new incipient federation.

The ancient Southern Super Continent (South America, Africa, Arabia, India before it moved to collide with Asia, Australia, and Antarctica) is now called *Gondwana*. Politically in the present it will have to unite by a separate process when it is ready.

A fused single supercontinent formed by the fusion of Laurasia and *Gondwana* is called *Pangea* – or "all of Earth". It would clearly be a world federation. I find one symbolic problem with this. Last time this happened in Late Permian times (255 million years ago), it triggered the biggest mass extinction in Earth history, with 96% of all then existing species gone. It would be wise to avoid those symbolic implications.

As for a capital for *Laurasia*, I propose Prague, as being almost exactly the mid-point of Europe. (The fact that I was born in Prague is purely coincidental. We all have our biases though.) It is an ancient capital, for a time in the Middle Ages the capital of the Holy Roman Empire. There Johannes Kepler and Tycho de Brahe launched the first serious scientific studies of astronomy. Charles University in Prague is one of the oldest universities in Europe (founded 1348). The 30 years' war in Europe began with the Prague defenestration of some Catholic ambassadors by Protestants. (Not that this is a good symbol for the future, but it does illustrate the central importance of Prague in European history). Finally in an old legend I learned in school, Libuse, the old woman ruler of Bohemia and founder of Prague, prophesied in one of her visions "I see a great city, whose glory will reach the stars". A good omen for a capital of *Laurasia*!

Catch That Runaway Metaphor

Laurasia United, Vancouver Vladivostok,
V for victory, nations together flock
In a future dream of East-West bridging
Not through land drifts, but through people dredging
Oceans of old distrust, quarrels of doubtful merit
Swept on by streams of hope, rushing to share it
Can it be done? If walls of brick can fall,
What limits outstretched hands when cousins call?

If Laurasia is One will Gondwana follow?
Yet fissures deep still rift a vexing furrow
Through the hot south, hot in sun and blood
And salty tears of grief, the trench may flood.
Pangea beckons from afar as final goal
Yet don't push this too far, for on this shoal
The Earth once nearly wrecked its living sphere
In Permian Extinction, to a thin veneer.

Lesson is simply: symbols pushed too hard
Obscure the message you wish to impart.

Notes

1. North Atlantic Treaty Organization, Warsaw Treaty Organization, European Community, European Free Trade Area, Council for Mutual Economic Cooperation, Conference on Security and Cooperation in Europe. See also the Glossary at the end of the first chapter, p. 30, for other acronyms.

PART II. — WAR PREVENTION

Components of an Active Peace Policy

DIETRICH FISCHER*

Only two countries in the world have been free from war since the time of Napoleon, Sweden and Switzerland (Small and Singer 1982). Both have maintained a strong conventional defence relative to their strategic importance, but have strictly observed the provision never to fight abroad (except for Sweden's participation in UN peacekeeping operations). This seems no coincidence. To prevent war, a country must make two things clear to a potential aggressor: (1) if he attacks, the costs will far outweigh the expected gains, and (2) as long as he does not attack, he has absolutely nothing to fear. The first point is widely heeded, but the second point is often overlooked, although it is no less important. Non-offensive defence emphasizes both points equally.

A strategy of non-offensive defence remains an important contribution to helping keep a country out of war, but in the future it will no longer be enough. If a war were to escalate to the use of nuclear weapons, even countries not directly involved could be totally destroyed. It is no longer enough to be prepared to resort to defence if a crisis should erupt into war. It has become necessary to pursue an active peace policy (Fischer *et al.* 1989) that seeks to anticipate potential conflicts and prevent or

* A longer version of this paper was presented at the Session on *Common Security: Moving from Confrontation to Cooperation* at the Sixth General Assembly of the World Future Society, Washington, DC, July 19, 1989, and published in Futures Research Quarterly, Fall 1990, Vol. 6, No. 3, p. 45-64.

resolve them long before they lead to war. Non-offensive defence, while an important component of an active peace policy, must be supplemented by a comprehensive set of economic, diplomatic and legal approaches aimed at creating a climate in which war becomes implausible. Another recent proposal for a comprehensive global security strategy, putting somewhat greater emphasis on seeking global agreements than on taking independent initiatives, is offered in Hollins *et al.* (1989).

An active peace policy has three main components: (1) cooperation, (2) conflict resolution, and (3) self-defence. Greater international cooperation, especially between countries with a history of mutual hostility, can create an atmosphere of better mutual understanding and trust, and an interest on both sides to maintain mutually beneficial relations. If conflicts erupt nevertheless, as they undoubtedly will from time to time, there exists a whole range of methods of conflict resolution to settle disputes without war. If an adversary refuses to resolve a conflict peace-

Table I. Ten Components of an Active Peace Policy

A. Conflict Prevention
    1 International cooperation

B. Conflict Resolution
    2 Unilateral concession
    3 Negotiation
    4 Good offices
    5 Mediation
    6 Arbitration
    7 International law

C. Self-defence
    8 Invulnerability
    9 Dissuasion
    10 Non-offensive defence

fully and resorts to aggression, non-military and non-offensive military defense can help resist aggression without leading to an escalation of war.

The following sections contain some brief observations about each of these three components of an active peace policy. Table I gives an overview of the methods discussed.

Cooperation

In the famous Robbers Cave experiment, social psychologist Muzafer Sherif and his associates have found that one of the most effective ways to overcome a climate of mutual hostility and distrust is for two groups to work together to achieve a superordinate goal, something that is in both sides' interest, but cannot be accomplished by either side alone (Sherif and Sherif 1969; Fischer *et al.* 1989, p. 17-18).

At the 1985 summit meeting in Geneva, Ronald Reagan said to Mikhail Gorbachev, if the earth was invaded by aliens, their two countries would surely become allies to fight them. But there is no need to wait for an invasion from outer space. There are plenty of problems right here on earth that can only be solved if the two superpowers and all major industrial countries cooperate: preventing destruction of the ozone layer, controlling the greenhouse effect, avoiding the spread of nuclear weapons to terrorist groups, and many more. As long as one single country makes nuclear weapons technology available to unstable governments or to terrorists, all countries will be in great danger. Global cooperation is indispensable to solve such problems.

There is a range of other problems where international cooperation is not absolutely necessary, but would be of great benefit to all involved, particularly in economic, cultural and scientific cooperation. If a new discovery has been made, the cost does not depend on the number of uses, but the benefits are far greater the more people have access to it. For this reason, international scientific cooperation brings all participants greater results at lower costs than separate efforts.

It was the genius of Claude Monnet to foresee that to overcome the century-old hostility between France and Germany, a mutually beneficial common institution would pave the way. He conceived of the Coal and Steel Union which benefited all the six initial members, including Germany and France. It became the nucleus out of which today's European Community developed. It has made war between France and Germany as unthinkable as the German unification of 1870 made war between Prussia and Bavaria unthinkable.

Similar projects are now required to begin a gradual dissolution of the East-West divide in Europe. The gas pipeline from Siberia to Western Europe is a good example of such a cooperative venture. The Reagan administration asserted that this pipeline would make Western Europe dependent on the Soviet Union and tried to block its construction. But the Soviet Union is as much interested in the reverse flow of hard currency as Western Europe is in the flow of gas. Besides, that gas represents only a small fraction of Western Europe's energy consumption. This project is mutually beneficial and increases both sides' stake in maintaining good relations. The following is a list of additional conceivable joint projects:

1. Joint research and development of processes to eliminate sulfur dioxide from coal burning plants to reduce acid rain and allow damaged forests to regenerate;

2. Exchange of information and joint research on pollution-free and low-polluting manufacturing processes;

3. Extending the TGV network of fast trains into a pan-European network, to encourage greater use of public transportation instead of private automobiles, helping curb air pollution. Joint adoption of stricter limits on automobile exhausts;

4. Increased exchange of students and teachers between East and West, and in general expanding the free flow of people, ideas and information across the East-West border, adding more telephone lines, developing joint computer networks,

exchange of printed material, radio and television programs, etc. An important first step is the adoption of compatible technologies with regard to computers, television, fibre optics etc.;

5. Expanding East-West Trade. There are great potential, mutual gains, not only from comparative advantage, but also from mutual specialization, making better use of potential scale economies in a larger market;

6. Cooperation on finding cures for cancer, AIDS and other diseases;

7. Joint exploration of outer space;

8. Common efforts to eliminate hunger and illiteracy in the Third World.

Every country should be invited to participate, but it is not necessary to wait until all are ready to join. Cooperation in some of these areas can set in motion a benign escalatory process. The more joint undertakings that have already succeeded, the greater is the mutual readiness to go further.

It is important to guard against disappointments in some of these undertakings, so as not to spoil a promising beginning. For example, rather than buying entire manufacturing plants from another country, joint ventures give a greater incentive to each side to make the undertaking succeed. China learned this through bitter experience. Among a number of complete plants it bought from abroad in the early 1970s was a steel rolling mill. After it had paid for the plant, it discovered that it was built on soft ground and the machines got out of alignment and did not work properly anymore. When it asked the construction firm to help fix the problem, it was told, "This plant now belongs to you and this is your responsibility". From then on, it relied increasingly on joint ventures, where the supplier of a plant is not paid in cash, but receives a certain share of the profits. Then the supplier will have every incentive to make sure that the plant remains in good working order at all times and that there is a market for the product, regardless of what is specified in the contract. Joint ventures between firms in East and West in a whole range of industries could increase the revenue of the firms involved, as well as reduce costs and improve the living standards of consumers on both sides.

It has been argued that Eastern Europeans might wish to buy a great deal from the West, but had relatively little to offer in return, because the quality of goods manufactured in Eastern Europe was not up to Western standards. The same could be said about Chinese products when China opened its borders to trade with the West in the early 1970s. Few people in the West were interested in buying grey Mao uniforms. But some Western textile manufacturers went to China and showed the Chinese what styles of clothing and quality standards were in demand in the West, and how they could be manufactured. The Chinese were eager to learn, and this process has not only brought clothes at low cost to Western consumers, but has also helped to improve the quality and increase the variety of textiles available in China. Similarly, if Eastern Europeans wish to learn how to produce more for export to the West , both sides can benefit from higher quality and lower prices.

Such international cooperation, which can create common interests and a climate of mutual understanding in which war becomes unlikely, is far from setting up a world government. Most issues would still be dealt with at national or local levels. Jan Tinbergen (in Tinbergen and Fischer 1987) has estimated that about 70 percent of the world's decisions (measured by expenditures) are made at the individual or household level, 15 percent of world GNP is spent by local governments and 15 percent by national governments. He suggested that about 3 percent of world GNP ought to be spent at the global level, to deal with problems that defy national solutions, such as disarmament, peacekeeping, saving the global environment, eliminating world hunger.

In choosing the optimal level for various types of decision, the principle of subsidiarity is a useful guideline: Each decision ought to be made at the lowest level that includes all those affected by it. If the level is lower than that, external effects are not taken into account, and people engage in too many activities that are harmful to others, and not enough activities that are beneficial to others. For example, policies concerning acid rain require international agreements. If they are made at the national level, too much will be spent for polluting activities and not enough for efforts to clean up the pollution, because damage caused in other countries will be ignored. On the other hand, if decisions are made at a higher level than necessary, this creates an avoidable source of conflict. If people make a wrong decision and suffer the consequences, they have only themselves to blame and will try to choose more wisely in the future. But if someone at the top of a bureaucratic chain made that decision for them and they suffer, they have reason to project their anger on the person responsible for the mistake. For example, if the ministry of agriculture orders a farmer to plant wheat when he knows that by planting tomatoes he could earn three times as much, he will have legitimate grievances. For this reason, excessively centralized, undemocratic systems are often filled with tension and may rely on political repression to keep disputes from erupting openly.

Conflict Resolution

When I once spoke before an American audience about the benefits of international cooperation, a military officer stood up and said, "You live in a world of illusions. As long as civilization exists, there will always be conflict," and from his grim expression it was clear that he meant armed conflict, or war.

Conflicts in the form of differences of opinion and interest will probably always emerge anew from time to time. But this does not mean that we have to kill each other to resolve them. IBM and the American Telephone and Telegraph Company are engaged in an intense struggle over the conquest of the computerized telecommunications market, but they would never dream of bombing each other's headquarters, or slaughtering each other's employees. There are more civilized ways to wage conflict, by competing with lower prices, better quality, and occasionally with battles in court.

The members of the European Community do have some conflicts among themselves, but have developed mechanisms to solve them nonviolently. When Great Britain complained that it had been overcharged with contributions to the EC, Margaret Thatcher negotiated with the heads of state of the other EC members, and an agreement was reached to reimburse Great Britain, not as much as it had sought, but by a reasonable amount. Nobody fired any guns. There is no reason why disputes between East and West cannot be settled in a similar manner, with some sanity on both sides.

One can distinguish between six approaches to conflict resolution, to deal with conflicts of increasing intractability:

1. unilateral concession;
2. negotiation;
3. good offices;
4. mediation;
5. arbitration;
6. court of law.

Method (1) involves only one of the parties to the conflict. Method (2) involves all the conflict parties (usually two). Methods (3) – (6) involve the conflict parties and an impartial outsider playing a gradually more intrusive role. A party providing good offices simply makes available a neutral meeting ground, or carries messages back and forth between two conflict parties without making any suggestions of its own. A mediator tries to come up with sensible compromise proposals, but leaves the decision whether to adopt them to the conflicting parties. An arbitrator makes the final decision, after both parties have pledged that they will voluntarily accept the verdict. A court of law, to be effective, may need the capacity to bring sanctions against a party that refuses to accept its decisions.

Brief examples may help illustrate how each of these six methods work. The idea is to begin with the first, and gradually go down the list if the previous method has failed to bring results.

Unilateral concession: When a fire at a chemical warehouse near Basel poisoned the Rhine river, killing fish and making drinking water unusable for many communities along the river in France, Germany and Holland, Switzerland did not wait to be taken to court, or even to negotiate with its neighbours over compensation. The Swiss government announced that it would pay for the cleanup, in an effort to defuse justified public anger.

Negotiations: As already mentioned, when Britain felt it had overpaid contributions to the EC, it negotiated a compensation.

Good Offices: Finland hosted the 1975 Conference on Security and Cooperation in Europe. Constructing Finlandia Hall in Helsinki, where the conference was held, was a good investment. It probably contributed far more to Finland's security than adding a new tank division to Finland's armed forces. Moreover, it did not threaten Finland's neighbours, but improved the security of all other European countries as well. It contributed to *common security*.

Mediation: An emissary of the Pope was able to mediate the dispute between Argentina and Chile over the Beagle Canal. UN General Secretary Perez de Cuellar mediated a cease-fire in the Iraq-Iran war. It is often easier for both parties to a dispute to accept a proposal made by a neutral party than a proposal made by the other side, because that might bring a loss of face before domestic public opinion.

Arbitration: When the US and Canada were unable to negotiate an agreement over fishing rights off their coasts, they submitted the dispute to a panel of judges from the World Court in The Hague, and both parties announced in advance that they would accept the judges' verdict, whatever it might be.

Court of Law: When France planned to end the special status of a duty-free zone surrounding Geneva, Switzerland took its case before the World Court, and France accepted the court's decision that it ought to maintain the zone. When the US mined Nicaragua's harbors, Nicaragua filed a complaint before the World Court and won. Unfortunately, the Reagan administration refused to accept the decision, and has in this way impaired the USs' own credibility if a future administration wishes to take international disputes before the World Court.

Countries can reduce the danger of war if they take international disputes that they cannot resolve by any of the other five methods to the World Court. It is best not to wait until a serious dispute erupts, but to practise that route now with relatively unimportant and non-controversial cases.

It is a welcome sign that the Soviet Union has accepted the World Court's jurisdiction over disputes involving five conventions on human rights: the prohibition of genocide, slavery, racism and torture, and the guarantee of political rights of women (New York Times, 9 March 1989). The US has ratified only one of these conventions, the prohibition of genocide, but specified that it would not submit to a ruling of the World Court in case of a dispute over its interpretation. Of course, the actual implementation of human rights is even more important than their formal adoption. But the USs' refusal to accept the jurisdiction of the World Court in such matters sets a bad example for other countries. The more countries rely on the World Court, and the greater the number of areas in which they accept its jurisdiction, the less likely it is that a given dispute will lead to war.

If we pursue an active peace policy, we do not simply wait until a conflict becomes acute and then resort to legal proceedings to solve it, but rather we seek negotiations over any disagreements at an early stage when it is generally much easier to find an amicable solution. In fact, in choosing topics for negotiations, it is best not to begin with highly contested issues, but with areas where there are clearly visible and immediate benefits to both sides (win-win solutions), such as increased trade, mutual sharing of civilian technology, and cultural exchanges. Success in those areas can create a climate of trust in which it will become possible to resolve more difficult disputes later. Ross Perot, a Texas oil billionaire, once criticized the Reagan administration's confrontational approach toward the Soviet Union by saying,

"If I sit down at the negotiating table and wish to strike a business deal, I don't begin by breaking the teeth of the person sitting across from me. That will not bring me any agreement. I search for common interest."

Political leaders might be able to learn from successful business people.

So far, there has been a strange asymmetry in law, both at the domestic and international level. It focuses exclusively on the prevention of wrongdoing through the threat of punishment or sanctions, but it entirely fails to encourage desirable behavior through the promise of rewards. One of the basic sources of problems in the world is the existence of what economists call "externalities," the fact that decision-makers often do not enjoy the good or suffer the bad consequences of their choices themselves. For this reason, too many actions tend to be taken that harm others and not enough that help others. Law seeks to deter actions that are harmful to others by punishing those who cause harm. But it fails to encourage people to do more for the benefit of society or of the international community by rewarding those who improve the lot of others. There is, in fact, some rudimentary approach to that problem. Someone who has discovered a new cure for a disease, or has made significant contributions to world peace, may receive a Nobel Prize. But this is as if once a year we were to punish "the criminal of the year" from around the world in an exemplary fashion, while every other criminal got away free. We would hardly consider this an adequate legal system. There is a need to develop what might be called "remunerative law", which rewards not just the victims of wrongdoing, but rather those who make sacrifices for the benefit of others and society as a whole, both at the domestic and international level, as a complement to the type of *penal law* that has already been developed to a modest extent. This is a great task waiting for us in the future.

Self-Defence

No matter how many precautions are taken to avert war in the first place, prudence requires us to be prepared against aggression if it should ever become necessary. In the long run, it is desirable to assign that task to a United Nations peacekeeping force. Until a sufficiently effective global peacekeeping force has been established, countries must rely on self-defence or collective self-defence.

Even this is not a purely military task. Self-defence includes three main components:

1. Invulnerability
2. Dissuasion
3. Non-offensive defence.

Invulnerability

Bomb shelters and underground hospitals are not really "weapons", but they can reduce loss of life if a country is attacked. A country can make itself less vulnerable by having a decentralized decision-making apparatus that cannot easily be "decapitated." Similarly, a dense, redundant transportation network with numerous alternative routes is much harder to disrupt than a highly streamlined network with only a few principal routes.

Reserves of food and other vital raw materials and stand-by plans to produce imported goods domestically can protect a country against an interruption of imports. It may be more expensive to produce such goods domestically than buying them on the world market, but it will be far less expensive than going to war. Rationing in cases of an emergency can help ensure that the most essential needs are covered.

During peacetime, Switzerland imports about 50 percent of the food it consumes, but it has a plan to become self-sufficient in food over three years if this should be necessary and keeps food reserves to bridge the gap until the plan can be put into effect (Fischer 1982; Zentralstelle für Gesamtverteidigung 1973, 1979).

There is a difference between complete autarchy and *self-reliance* or potential self-sufficiency if needed. Self-reliant is someone who keeps some candles in the house in case the electricity is cut off. Autarchy is practised by someone who uses only candles for fear that electricity might be cut off some day.

Self-reliance is perfectly compatible with a high volume of mutually beneficial trade in peacetime. But it eliminates one potential source of war, conflict over sources of raw materials, such as oil from the Near East.

Dissuasion

This strategy seeks to avert war by convincing a potential aggressor, without evoking fear, that peaceful cooperation serves his interests better than going to war. To this end, a country can make peace more attractive and war less attractive. Peace can be made more attractive by increasing the benefits from mutual cooperation and by voluntarily removing injustices an adversary may perceive to suffer in peacetime. Similarly, war can be made less attractive by increasing the losses an aggressor would suffer, and by reducing any benefits he might hope to gain. This yields four components of a comprehensive strategy of dissuasion (Galtung 1968; Fischer 1984). Military defense focuses on only one of the four, inflicting greater losses on an aggressor, but neglects the other three. The following are some brief examples of methods of dissuasion.

Inflicting losses on an aggressor is usually seen as a military task. But even here, nonmilitary methods can be effective. It has been said that the construction of a United Nations office complex outside Vienna saved Austria two divisions. A country that invaded Austria would probably earn the enmity of 150 nations around the world whose diplomats might be harmed.

To reduce the gains an aggressor might expect, one can deny an occupation force control over the population and economic resources. Sweden threatened to blow up the hydroelectric dams supplying its iron ore and coal mines in case of a German invasion, which would have made them unusable for years. Switzerland threatened to blow up its bridges and Alpine tunnels. Nonviolent resistance has proven effective in several instances, even though it has been only spontaneous and never been planned, exercised and funded as much as military defence. Nobody can govern a country unless its citizens cooperate voluntarily to some degree. If a soldier needs to stand next to every worker, a country becomes effectively ungovernable (Sharp 1985).

Wilhein Nolte (in Fischer *et al.* 1989) proposes the concept of *autonomous protection*, a combination of civilian-based defense in cities with non-offensive conventional defence in rural areas. He starts with the observation that during World War II those cities that had important military installations were generally bombed, while demilitarized cities were largely spared and provided a safe haven for refugees from the fighting in the countryside. Therefore, trying to defend population centers with military means invites their destruction.

To increase the benefits from peaceful cooperation, a country can deliberately seek to make itself useful to its neighbours as long as left in peace. Some have argued that what helped Switzerland stay out of World War II was not so much its defence (meaning military defence), but lucky circumstances, like the fact that both sides in the war needed a neutral place for banking transactions and exchange of information. But documents about Swiss defence plans reveal that this was not pure luck. It was a deliberate aspect of a comprehensive security policy that sought to persuade everyone that invading the country would not advance but hurt their interests. Who would wish to bombard his or her own bank account?

To reduce any losses an opponent might perceive to suffer in peacetime, a country need not wait until complaints are lodged.

It can seek to anticipate potential sources of grievance and remove them before they develop into an open conflict. From this perspective, the former Rumanian dictator Ceausescu's plan to raze small hamlets among Rumania's Hungarian minority and combine them into larger towns against those people's wishes was highly provocative. The new government has wisely abandoned that plan. When Teheran prohibited the use of Arabic at schools in the Arabic-speaking province of Khuzistan bordering on Iraq, with bloody riots as a result, this was one more factor that tempted Iraq to attack Iran. Treating minorities well is an important component of an active peace policy.

Non-offensive Defence

If dissuasion fails to change the mind of the would-be aggressor, the last resort is to physically prevent him from attacking. At the same time it is important to avoid that defense preparations be misperceived as a threat to an opponent. Otherwise the opponent may feel under pressure to eliminate that threat if war seems imminent. A typical example is Egypt's development of an air force under President Nasser. He believed this would make Egypt militarily stronger and therefore more secure. But in fact it created an unstable situation in which the outbreak of war became more likely. Both Egypt and Israel possessed vulnerable bomber fleets on unprotected airfields in the desert. Each side knew that in case of war, whoever struck first could destroy the other side's air force on the ground. Thus, when tensions increased in 1967, Israel felt so terrified by Egypt's air force that it felt it had no choice but to destroy it in a surprise attack, before it could be used against Israel. Sweden and Switzerland deliberately did not acquire any long-range bombers before World War II, because they feared that possessing such weapons might invite a preemptive air attack, rather than deterring it. Instead, they concentrated on short-range interceptors and anti-aircraft defences (Roberts, 1986).

The threat to escalate a conventional war to nuclear war might conceivably help deter a conventional attack if the only way in which a war could ever begin was through deliberate aggression. But not every war in history has started with a deliberate attack like Hitler's march into Poland in 1939. War War I was triggered by a shot fired by an individual assassin at Sarajevo. It is not even always obvious which side really started a war. In the Vietnam war, the United States and North Vietnam both saw each other as the aggressor. Israel maintains that Egypt started the 1967 Mideast war by blocking Israeli ships at the Bay of Aqaba. Egypt maintains that Israel started the war by subsequently bombing Egyptian air fields. It is always possible to find something the other side did first. If a war, begun for whatever reason, is then escalated to the use of nuclear weapons, it is likely to lead to the total destruction of both sides. NATO's current doctrine of flexible response, which foresees the first use of nuclear weapons to deter a conventional attack, is as if we tried to prevent traffic accidents by packing our own car full of dynamite, putting a trip wire around it and telling everybody, "Don't hit us, or our car will explode and kill you" (and us too, of course). This should indeed deter anyone from hitting us intentionally. But if we have the slightest collision for any other reason, it is our end.

To prevent war, it is important to oppose aggression firmly but not to overreact. Before World War I, the prevailing view was that the best way to avoid war was to be prepared to win it. The key to victory was seen to be quick and decisive action at the outset of a war to surprise and defeat the adversary's forces before they could be fully mobilized. As a result of this philosophy, the world became rapidly engulfed in the conflagration of World War I, sparked by the events at Sarajevo.

From that experience many concluded that avoiding war required a more conciliatory attitude. Chamberlain probably thought he had learnt the lessons of Sarajevo when he yielded to Hitler's demands in Munich in 1938. As we now know, the consequences were even worse.

After World War II, the pendulum has swung back full cycle: Emphasizing the risks of appeasement, both NATO and the now dissolved Warsaw Treaty Organization vowed that they would react strongly to the first signs of aggression. By threatening strong retaliation and deliberate escalation, such strategies seek to deter intentional aggression. But they fail to prevent wars through accident or miscalculation. Remembering Munich, both sides seem to have forgotten the lessons of Sarajevo.

Non-offensive defence can avoid both types of war: by maintaining a strong defense, it can credibly resist the type of aggression with which World War II began. Yet by avoiding preparations for offensive operations into the territory of an opponent, it helps prevent the automatic escalation of fighting that led to World War I.

There are some who claim that it is impossible to distinguish between offensive and defensive arms. Whether a weapon is offensive or defensive depends entirely on its intended use, they argue. For example, when Mikhail Gorbachev, in a speech to the United Nations in December 1988, announced a restructuring of Soviet forces to a more clearly defensive military posture, Henry Kissinger commented,

"When they say they are shifting to a defensive posture, nobody really knows what that means precisely. For example, a tank has been called an offensive weapon. But it is also said that the best defence against a tank is a tank . ... "

Of course, there exist some borderline cases of arms that can be used either in a defensive or offensive way. But there also exist arms that can be classified unambiguously. For example, a tank barrier in a fixed position cannot be used to invade another country. A first strike weapon, such as a bomber on an unprotected airfield, which would have to be used first in combat or else it would be lost, has practically only offensive uses. To cite one example in order to claim that such a distinction cannot be made is as if someone were to say, "There is no distinction between light and dark colors. Take for example grey, it is neither light nor dark . ... "

If two potential adversaries adopt a posture of *mutual defensive superiority*, then each side is able to defend itself if necessary, but unable to win an attack against the other side, and the risk of war, even during periods of tension and conflict, is greatly diminished.   '

Concluding Observations

Modern science and technology have given humanity unprecedented capabilities for good or evil. Automation and robotization promise to increase our production potential enormously and potentially help eliminate hunger and poverty. Solar energy can free us from dependence on exhaustible fuel supplies. A network of glass fiber cables criss-crossing the globe may permit instant communication between people anywhere. Computerized question-answering systems may give doctors or teachers access to the knowledge of the world's leading specialists. We possess the know-how to eradicate diseases entirely, but have so far largely failed to make use of it. Smallpox was eradicated at a cost of $80 million, half the cost of a single MX missile. A campaign to eradicate malaria, from which millions suffer, has been estimated to cost $300 million, roughly 2 percent of the cost of one aircraft carrier task force. For the first time, we have a realistic chance to overcome the scourges that have plagued humanity since the dawn of history.

On the other hand, we have acquired the capacity to turn the earth into a radioactive wasteland. We can alter the climate so that lush forests turn into deserts and many densely populated coastal regions become immersed by a rising sea level, and we are in the process of doing so. We cause the extinction of plant and animal species at a much faster rate than during the period when the dinosaurs and many other forms of life died out. We are rapidly using up exhaustible resources that have accumulated over millions of years. We are depleting the ozone layer that protects us from cancer-causing ultraviolet radiation.

In the past, human capacity to destroy the environment was so limited that we had the luxury to wait until damage became visible and then to react with corrective measures. People could afford to learn through trial and error.

Today, a single error can be fatal. We cannot afford to burn fossil fuels until the greenhouse effect melts the polar icecaps and we can observe the sea level rising. At that point, it would already be too late to reverse the trend. We cannot afford a single nuclear war, deliberate or accidental.

The way our political systems now generally operate, by reacting to problems *after* they have become manifest, is comparable to driving a car with closed eyes. We wait until we feel that we have hit the edge of the road, and then take corrective action to get back onto the pavement. At a slow speed and with no other vehicles on the road, it may be possible to operate that way, although it is not very efficient. But at high speed on a crowded road, such a strategy is fatal. We must now begin to look into the future to try to foresee the dangers waiting for us before they hit us, and take corrective action to avoid them in time. We must make every effort to prevent wars before they occur, rather than focussing our attention on how to fight wars once they happen.

Let us drive with open eyes.

Notes

Fischer, Dietrich (1982) *Invulnerability Without Threat: The Swiss Concept of General Defense*, Journal of Peace Research Vol. 19, No. 3, p. 205-225.

Fischer, Dietrich (1984) *Preventing War in the Nuclear Age* Totowa, New Jersey: Rowman & Allanheld.

Fischer, Dietrich, Wilhelm Nolte and Jan Oberg (1989) *Winning Peace: Strategies and Ethics for a Nuclear-Free World.* New York and London: Taylor & Francis.

Fisher, Roger, and William Ury (1981) *Getting to Yes: Negotiating Agreement Without Giving In.* Boston: Houghton Mifflin.

Galtung, Johan (1968) *On the Strategy of Nonmilitary Defense: Some Proposals and Problems* in Bartels, ed., *Peace and Justice: Unity or Dolemma.* Institute of Peace Research , Catholic University of Nijmegen. Reprinted in Johan Galtung, Essays in Peace Research, vol. 2 Copenhagen: Eljers, 1976, p. 378-426.

Galtung, Johan (1984) *There are Alternatives! Four Roads to Peace and Security*. Nottingham: Spokesman.

Gorbachev, Mikhail (1987a) *The Reality and Guarantee of a Secure World* Pravda, September 17. Official translation released by the Soviet Mission to the United Nations, News York.

Gorbachev, Mikhail (1987b) *Perestroika: New Thinking for Our Country and the World*. New York: Harper and Row.

Hollins, Harry B., Averill L. Powers and Mark Sommer (1989) *The Conquest of War: Alternative Strategies for Global Security*, Boulder, Colorado, and London: Westview.

Roberts, Adam (1986) *Nations in Arms: The Theory and Practice of Territorial Defense* 2nd ed. New York: St. Martin's.

Sharp, Gene (1985) *Making Europe Unconquerable: the Potential of Civilian-Based Deterrence and Defence.* Cambridge, Mass.: Ballinger.

Sherif, Muzafer and Carolyn Sherif (1969) *Social Psychology.* New York: Harper and Row.

Small, Melvin and J. David Singer (1982) *Resort to Arms: International and Civil Wars, 1816-1980.* Newbury Park, CA: Sage.

Tinbergen, Jan and Dietrich Fischer (1987) *Warfare and Welfare: Integrating Security Policy into Socio-Economic Policy.* Brighton: Wheatsheaf, New York: St. Martin's Press.

Implementation of Arms Control Treaties

DOUGLAS SCOTT *

The Markland Group in Hamilton, Ontario, is concerned with disarmament, but we are different from some other groups in the field in that we do not advocate anything in the nature of unilateral disarmament,. We do not support anything like banning cruise missiles or withdrawing from NATO. We believe disarmament can only occur, and should only occur, through the making of treaties. Unilateral gestures may help to get the process started, but if it is to continue, and if there is to be no backsliding, there must be treaties.

We will start by looking at some examples of the type of arms control treaties that there are on the books thus far. In 1972, the Anti-Ballistic Missile (ABM) Treaty was signed. This is the treaty that is hampering the United States in its Strategic Defence Initiative (SDI) program. In 1987, the Intermediate Nuclear Forces (INF) Treaty was signed which marked the first time that the Soviets permitted on-site inspection of their territory.

These are both bilateral treaties in the sense that they involve only the two superpowers, or only the two alliances, NATO and Warsaw Treaty Organization.

But there is another type of treaty, which we believe to be even more important, and that is the multilateral treaty. These are the ones that are intended to be signed by as many countries as can be persuaded. There are fourteen treaties in this category and

---

* Modified from a talk to the Rotary Club in Hamilton in 1989. This material has been expanded upon and thoroughly documented in the book *Disarmament's Missing Dimension* by the Markland Policy Group (Science for Peace / Samuel Stevens 1990) 150pp.

more are under negotiation. An example of a multilateral treaty is the Nuclear Test Ban Treaty which was signed in 1963. It bans nuclear tests in the atmosphere, in outer space and under water – everywhere except underground. It has about 110 parties out of a total of 165 countries in the world. Another of these multilateral treaties is the Non-Proliferation Treaty which was signed in 1968 and has about 150 parties. It is intended to prevent nuclear weapons from spreading to countries other than the five countries that had them in 1968, namely the US, the UK, the Soviet Union, France and China.

In addition to these two treaties, there are a number of regional treaties, and also treaties covering specific weapons, such as land mines and sea-bed weapons. Again, these are all multilateral treaties.

The reason we in The Markland Group regard the multilateral treaties as being so important is that arms control is essentially an ongoing process. The way things are developing, it looks as if there will be a whole series of these multilateral treaties – each covering a different category of weapons, or possibly a different group of countries. At the present time there are discussions going on relating to a number of new treaties: there is one covering chemical weapons, one for radiological weapons, outer space weapons, missile technology, military budget controls, and a comprehensive nuclear test ban.

All of these treaties will be multilateral treaties. We foresee this trend as continuing until there is a whole network of these treaties. At some point in this process, the world will start to experience a really significant degree of disarmament.

If you believe , as we do, that the process of disarmament consists of the making of a series of multilateral treaties, you will understand why we think this type of treaty is just as important, if not more important, than the bilateral treaties. It is true that at the early stages of the process, the bilateral treaties are very important. But eventually, all the arms control treaties will have to be multilateral – even the treaties covering strategic nuclear weapons.

Our interest in multilateral treaties, however, is not so much centred on what kind of weapons they cover or who signs them. What we are interested in is the part of the treaty that deals with verification and compliance.

We concentrate exclusively on the framework: the part that is intended to persuade the parties to comply and prevent the treaty from disintegrating. Unless there is a strong framework available for these multilateral treaties, there will be very few countries that are prepared to sign them. And if a treaty *is* signed with a weak framework, that treaty is quite likely to fall apart. We believe that the whole disarmament process depends on having a strong framework for multilateral treaties.

It was for this reason that we decided to examine very closely the type of verification framework in use under the various arms control treaties.

In the case of the bilateral treaties, we found a very simple verification system. It consists of clauses whereby the two parties – in this case the two superpowers – agree to submit to certain types of inspection and surveillance –sometimes by satellite and sometimes by on-site inspection. That system seems to be working well enough – or at least there have been no treaties lost as a result of a breakdown in the verification system. Also, the two superpowers show no inclination to alter it or to adopt a different type of system.

In the case of the multilateral treaties, which are the ones that are so important in the disarmament process, we found that this simple type of system is not used. It seems that these treaties need something that is much broader in scope. We can get an idea what a broad-scope type of system looks like in a multilateral treaty by looking at the Non-Proliferation Treaty, the NPT.

The verification framework in the NPT contains four elements. The first consists of the same kind of clause that we find in the bilateral treaties, namely, a clause stating what type of inspection and surveillance the parties are required to submit to.

Secondly, the NPT provides for an international agency, and gives this agency the responsibility for conducting the inspections and administering the surveillance system. That agency, called the International Atomic Energy Agency (IAEA), has headquarters in Vienna, and it sends out inspectors all over the world to count the fuel rods in the various nuclear power plants. If there are any missing, the assumption is that they have been diverted for the purpose of making nuclear weapons.

Thirdly, the treaty gives the agency in Vienna authority to make a decision as to whether a party has violated the treaty. This is the evaluation phase of the verification process.

Fourthly, in the event that the agency does make a formal decision that a violation has occurred, the agency is empowered to take certain measures for the purpose of persuading the delinquent states to rectify the violation. Under the NPT, there is a list of these persuasion measures that the agency is entitled to use, and it includes some rather mild sanctions. This type of clause is sometimes referred to as the response clause.

These are the four elements of the broad-scope type of verification system: the inspection and surveillance clauses, the agency clauses that establish the structure of the agency, the evaluation clauses and finally the response clauses. In addition, several other devices have been proposed for promoting compliance under multilateral treaties. These might be referred to as supplementary compliance devices, and they might comprise a fifth element in the broad-scope type of system. These will not be dealt with in this paper.

Now I want to compare this broad-scope type of system with the system used under the bilateral treaties. Under these bilateral treaties, the parties themselves look after the process of collecting the data relating to compliance. There is no international agency that operates the satellites or sends out the inspectors. Also the parties themselves do the evaluation. There is no agency that decides when the evidence adds up to a violation. When there is a violation indicated, again, the parties themselves take whatever steps they think appropriate in an effort to persuade the other side to rectify the situation. As you can see, the system used in the bilateral treaties depends entirely on the principle of self-help.

What we found therefore were two fundamentally different systems in effect: a self-help type of system in the bilateral treaties and a broad-scope type of system in the NPT.

A broad-scope type of system is obviously the more important one, because it is the one that is going to be needed for all the multilateral treaties, and it is the one that the whole process of disarmament is going to rely upon.

It seemed to us, therefore, to be important to examine how this broad-scope system was performing under the NPT. To begin with, we were reassured because the NPT has been a successful treaty. The problems in the area of non-proliferation have been with countries that have not signed the treaty: Israel, South Africa, Argentina, Brazil, India and Pakistan. The treaty itself is working.

We began to have our doubts about the effectiveness and acceptability of the multilateral treaty system because we noticed that it was not being used in most of the other multilateral treaties. Out of a total of 14 multilateral treaties, 11 are almost completely lacking in clauses providing for verification and compliance. We call them the 11 lame-duck treaties. When we discovered this situation, we began to think that there may be something wrong with the NPT verification system, even though that treaty has a good compliance record. It seemed to us that either the system was considered too weak or it was unacceptable for other reasons. Our doubts have been confirmed by some recent events.

This whole question of a verification framework for multilateral treaties has come up in connection with the new Chemical Weapons Convention (CWC). That treaty is now being negotiated by a UN committee in Geneva consisting of forty countries – the Conference on Disarmament – known as the CD.

The negotiating parties at the CD in Geneva started by looking at the verification system in the NPT. They quickly concluded that that system in the forms set out in the Non-Proliferation Treaty is *too vague*. These negotiators recognize that the self-help system won't work, and that the broad-scope type of system is probably what is required, but as for transplanting the particular system in the NPT into the CWC, they recognize that this cannot be done because it is lacking in detail. In fact when you look at it closely, it turns out to be nothing but a skeleton. Even though it works for the NPT the negotiators at the CD have concluded that a vast amount of work is going to be needed before that basic skeleton can be elaborated to the point were it can be put into a new chemical weapons treaty.

The same is true for all the other multilateral treaties; they all need a broad-scope system that is much more elaborate than any yet designed.

What all this means is that the world has not yet developed an adequate verification system for multilateral treaties. We find it difficult to understand why the governments of the world have neglected the task of constructing this system. It was needed for the eleven lame-duck treaties. It is needed now for the Chemical Weapons Convention. It will be needed for all the new multilateral treaties that are coming down the line. And yet, the basic preparatory work simply has not been done. There is no effective and acceptable verification system available to be incorporated into the various multilateral disarmament treaties.

Fortunately, the negotiating governments at the CD have recently started working on the problem. These governments are attempting to devise a strong verification system for the CWC. But given the lead-time needed before that system can be agreed upon and made operational, they should have started years ago. The reason these matters were neglected for so long is that the superpowers for a long time were opposed to the whole idea of the broad-scope type of verification system. They wanted nothing to do with an agency. They preferred the self-help type. So, for many years, there was no discussion at the CD about an agency or the mechanisms for persuading a country to comply.

Even now, there is virtually nothing being done towards developing this type of system, except at the CD in connection with the CWC. Unfortunately, there is a big problem at the CD. One or both of the superpowers are arguing for a verification system in which the agency has very limited powers – a system that still depends largely on the principle of self-help. We believe such a system would be too weak to hold the treaty together.

What is especially troubling is that the middle and smaller powers at the CD are sitting back and waiting for the superpowers to agree on something stronger. Middle powers like Canada, who favour a stronger system, should start designing the type of system they prefer. It is time to start working out the details since nobody has done this so far. They should then campaign for acceptance of their strong version of a verification system. If the superpowers cannot be persuaded to accept this version, it could nonetheless be incorporated in the Treaty, but with a clause that would allow the superpowers to opt out of the aspects of the system that they found unacceptable. In this event, the Treaty's strong verification system would apply to all signatories except those who had signed an opting-out declaration.

There are precedents for this type of arrangement, and although it is not ideal, it does work, and it is certainly better than the alternative, which is for the treaty to contain a watered-down verification system. The superpowers are still clinging to the principle of self-help; they are not yet ready to put their trust in an agency. That position should be respected, but it should not be allowed to prevent the rest of the world from putting into effect a system that is tailored to their needs – the needs of the countries that are not in a position to protect their interests by their own efforts and need the help of a strong international agency.

If the superpowers are ever to be persuaded to abandon the principle of self-help, it will only be as a result of seeing the other kind of system in operation and being convinced that it has more to offer.

Postscript December 1991

Since this speech was delivered in 1989, the situation has changed somewhat, although rather less than one might expect. The position of the Soviet Union is fluid. The US is still arguing for clauses that will weaken the treaty. Unfortunately, it has collected a number of supporters from among the group of countries previously known as the non-aligned. The countries that favour a stronger treaty have still not come together to formulate the type of system they prefer. They seem to be waiting for the US and its supporters to indicate that they would be prepared to discuss something stronger.

Meanwhile, the world still lacks an effective and acceptable compliance system for multilateral disarmament treaties. The Markland Group is attempting to organize an international academic workshop on this topic which would discuss the problems involved in designing such a system. The specific purpose of the workshop would be to alert the academic community to the problem and to encourage them to assist with the solution.

The United Nations Institute for Disarmament Research (UNIDIR) has agreed to cooperate with The Markland Group in organizing this workshop. Efforts are now underway to secure the funding.

UN Should Verify Arms Control Treaties

A. WALTER DORN *

The UN role in arms control is confined to discussion and negotiation. But as disarmament prospects have brightened and proposals have multiplied, many members feel it is time for the
United Nations to play a more active part by creating a UN system to verify treaties. Proponents include the Soviet Union,
which has said that the United Nations needs an agency that can
employ sophisticated tools, including a satellite monitoring capability and a worldwide system of seismic stations. The US, in
opposing a UN agency, has stressed that new treaties require
specific sets of verification measures which an agency is unlikely
to anticipate.

In 1988, members of the "Six-Nation Initiative" – Argentina,
Greece, India, Mexico, Sweden, and Tanzania – proposed that
the General Assembly commission a report outlining a UN
verification system. This proposal was merged with another
resolution drafted by Canada, France and the Netherlands. The
result was a final resolution asking the Secretary-General to
prepare a comprehensive report on the role of the United Nations
in verification. The Secretary-General's study, which was
undertaken with the assistance of governmental experts from 20
countries, was delivered to the General Assembly at the 1990 fall
session. Although most members favor the creation of a UN
verification arm, the Secretary-General's report did not make an
outright recommendation. The report reflected many of the

* Reprinted from the Bulletin of the Atomic Scientists, copyright © 1990
by the Educational Foundation of Nuclear Science, 6042 South Kimbark,
Chicago, IL 60637, USA.

arguments that have been made during the long debate at the United Nations over verification of arms control agreements.

In 1946, the US proposed the Baruch plan for the control of atomic energy. This plan would have created a powerful control agency. The Soviet Union rejected the Baruch proposal, interpreting it as a means of assuring that the US would retain its nuclear-weapons monopoly.

For nearly twenty years, disarmament negotiations remained deadlocked. The East charged that the West wanted "control without disarmament," and the West charged that the East wanted "disarmament without control." The US was unwilling to disarm without a system that could detect and punish violators, but the Soviets were unwilling to allow inspection of their secret military installations until after disarmament was assured. The Soviets wanted only verification of disarmament proper, regarding monitoring of existing armaments as legalized espionage. But the US considered monitoring essential in order to check that accepted limits were not exceeded.

In a dramatic policy reversal the Soviet Union has now accepted intrusive and wide-ranging international inspections – in some cases even before disarmament negotiations are completed. And at the Third UN Special Session on Disarmament in 1988, Soviet Foreign Minister Eduard Shevardnadze proposed the creation of an "international monitoring and verification agency" under UN auspices. He suggested that a "multilateral center to assist in verification" be established under the Secretary-General for "rendering assistance in verification matters to the parties of bilateral and regional agreements". During the 1988 regular session, he cited "the acute need for new mechanisms of verification and control", including a worldwide seismic monitoring system and an international satellite monitoring agency.

The US, on the other hand, now opposes a UN verification agency. It cast the single negative vote against the resolution initiating the Secretary-General's study and expressed the view that verification must be developed and agreed to by negotiating parties. The US

"did not see how the Secretary-General could undertake an in-depth study of the role of the United Nations in the field of verification in the abstract, in the absence of any parameters that specific agreements might provide for such a role in individual cases".[1]

Although the UK expressed the same view, it supported the resolution, declaring that a study of verification issues would nonetheless be useful.

Canada, the main driving force behind the development of verification resolutions in the General Assembly, has taken a progressive but cautious approach. Canada has sought a variety of verification measures short of a comprehensive agency, and has expressed the view that separate verification organizations created under different treaties might serve as stepping stones to the development of a single agency. Most NATO countries and Japan hold similarly cautious views.

Nearly all other member nations support UN-sponsored verification. The heads of state of 102 nonaligned nations recently endorsed the "establishment of an integrated multilateral verification system" within the framework of the United Nations.[2]

An effective UN verification agency would offer a number of advantages:

1. *Speed in treaty implementation.* If international expertise is available before a treaty is signed, a verification system can be in place when most needed – when treaty implementation begins. An example is the International Atomic Energy Agency's safeguards system, which was in place before the 1968 Non-Proliferation Treaty was signed and it is now involved in verification of two other treaties; the safeguards system was quickly extended to cover the treaty. Similarly, an existing agency could not only hasten treaty implementation, but agency experts might also be able to assist negotiators in drafting specific provisions.

2. *Cost.* An agency that verifies a number of treaties can save costs by sharing many scientific, technical and administrative resources. Since satellite data would be used to verify a number of treaties, the agency could employ a single team of expert image- and photo-interpreters[3]. Since verification costs would be spread over a longer time period, an existing agency might also flatten the "funding bubble" that treaties can create – the extraordinary costs incurred at the beginning of disarmament, when weapons are destroyed and verification begins. Much of the cost of personnel and institutional machinery involved in negotiating and maintaining a new agency for each treaty would also be eliminated.

3. *Protection of intelligence gathering.* A nation that obtains evidence of a treaty violation or suspicious activity may not wish to reveal its intelligence sources, although it may want the matter investigated by an objective body. If a UN agency investigated possible acts of noncompliance on request, the requesting state would not have to reveal the details of its sources or its "national technical means", such as secret satellite monitoring methods.

4. *Confidence.* The many peace-keeping and peace-making functions entrusted to the United Nations demonstrate that the nations of the world have confidence in the impartiality and objectivity of the Secretary-General and the UN Secretariat. A verification agency would allow nations with little experience or expertise to exercise their right to know if other parties to a treaty are in compliance. Furthermore, by involving the United Nations in verification, a civilian role would be assured.

Former UN Under-Secretary-General Dag Hammarskjold urged that any agency overseeing multilateral disarmament be part of the United Nations. Otherwise, he said, there would be "a hollowing out of the UN of one of its main fields of activity ".[4]

A number of existing multilateral treaties contain no effective verification provisions. These include the 1925 Geneva Protocol banning the use in war of chemical and biological weapons, the 1963 Partial Test Ban Treaty, the 1971 Sea-Bed Treaty (which prohibits placing nuclear weapons on the ocean floor), and the 1972 Biological Weapons Convention. A chemical weapons convention, a comprehensive test ban, and other anticipated arms limitation and disarmament agreements will require international verification. Future nuclear-weapon-free and demilitarized zones could benefit from a UN verification agency, and nations undertaking unilateral disarmament measures might request that the agency confirm their actions. If it were appropriate, the activities of the agency could also be expanded to include verification of cease-fire agreements, assistance with peace-keeping operations, and implementation of a global open skies plan.

Opponents of a UN verification agency argue that specific measures must be designed by the parties to each treaty. But the agency would have sufficient flexibility to respond to all requests by the negotiating parties. It could have separate divisions to develop special expertise covering the provisions of individual treaties. Each treaty would still be overseen by its own parties, who could meet regularly with agency officials to discuss compliance. The costs for each treaty-specific division could be borne by the parties to the treaty, while the overhead costs of the agency would be a part of UN membership fees.

Treaty compliance is the most sensitive issue in arms control. A UN agency need not automatically be given authority to evaluate compliance; decisions based on agency fact-finding could potentially be made at any level – an executive council of states overseeing the treaty, the agency's director, or the Secretary-General, or by each party individually. However, the agency should at least be able to express an opinion or make recommendations, since the agency's scientists and staff would probably be regarded as the most objective judges of the facts when a treaty violation is suspected.

A UN verification agency could meet the demand for effective multilateral arms control in coming decades. While bilateral agreements between the superpowers may continue to be based on adversarial inspection and surveillance, regional and global treaties require a strong multilateral framework for verification. The Secretary-General has recently been given a mandate to develop verification capability for the Geneva Protocol, which might be an appropriate first task for the agency.

A UN verification agency is the best means to develop an effective, treaty-specific, flexible, and objective system of multilateral verification, one which avoids wasteful duplication and can grow over time. The Secretary-General's report should encourage the evolution of such an agency and lay the foundation for a vital UN contribution to progressive disarmament and a safer world.

Notes

1. *United Nations Disarmament Yearbook 1988* (New York: United Nations, 1989) p. 368.

2. Final documents of the *Ninth Conference of Heads of State or Government of the Movement of Non-Aligned Countries*, Belgrade, September 1989.

3. A. Walter Dorn, *"Peace-keeping Satellites: The Case for International Surveillance and Verification"*, Peace Research Reviews, vol. 10 (May and June, 1987).

4. Brian Urquhart, *Hammarskjold* (New York: Knopf, 1972), p. 325.

PART III. — GLOBAL DECISION-MAKING

Binding Authority for the UN and Other International Organizations in Limited Functional and Territorial Fields

FINN SEYERSTED*

The present powers of the UN and their limitations

The best guarantee for peace is a strong international organization with powers of binding decisions and of military enforcement against aggression. If we survive, we will probably have that one day.

The United Nations is a beginning. Under the Charter the Security Council has these powers and can exercise them by a qualified majority vote (nine out of its fifteen members). But the power of the veto which the Charter confers upon the five big powers has in many cases prevented the Council from utilizing its powers. And the provisions on military action in articles 42 ff of the Charter have never been implemented or used – because of the veto.

The General Assembly may make decisions by a simple or two-thirds majority – and there is no power of veto. But the General Assembly can only make non-binding recommendations to the member states.

* Reprinted from Nordic Journal of International Law, Vol. 56, No. 3, 1987.

How can we get states to agree to abandon these limitations? More specifically: How can we get the big powers to accept a power of binding decisions without veto?

Weighted voting

The first condition for a strong international organization is a more realistic voting system.

The present system in the UN and most other international organizations is "one nation one vote", which implies that a state of 100,000 inhabitants has the same voting weight as a state of 1,000,000,000 inhabitants. This may be acceptable for recommendations which states can ignore and which they unfortunately frequently do ignore. But for binding decisions the big powers will not accept being outvoted by a two-thirds majority of small states, as has happened several times. The veto power is a very arbitrary means of avoiding this. Any one of the five big powers which took part in the founding of the UN has an absolute right to prevent a binding decision, whereas all the other big states have no stronger voting power than very small states.

The solution must be found in a system of weighted voting, where each state is accorded a voting power according to its population, its contribution to the budget of the organization and/or to other relevant criteria. There should be neither "one state one vote", nor voting strength in proportional to population or other criteria – but a compromise between the two: More voting strength for the big powers, but no veto for any one.

We already have that system in some organizations which have the power of making binding decisions: thus in two specialized agencies of the United Nations – the International Bank and the International Monetary Fund – each member has 250 votes plus an additional number of votes proportional to its paid-in quota of the capital stock (with some further adjustments in the case of the Fund) (see article XII, section 5 of the constitution of the Fund and article V, section 3 of the constitution of the Bank). This gives, in the Bank, the US 19.29%, the Nordic countries 3.48% and Bhutan 0.03%.

In international organizations which provide satellites for international telecommunications – such as INTELSAT, INMARSAT, and EUTELSAT – the members vote on substantive matters in proportion to their capital investment shares in the organization, which in turn are adjusted regularly in proportion to their utilization of the system (see e.g. INMARSAT Convention of 3 September 1976, art. 14 and the Operating Agreement of the same date, art. V, which provide in principle for an upward limit of 25% for any one member). Art. IX (i)(j) of the INTELSAT Constitution of 20 August 1971 provides that substantive decisions of the Board of Governors shall be taken either by at least four "governors" (i.e. national representatives) having at least two-thirds of the total voting participation (based on investment shares) – or by all members of the Board minus three, regardless of the voting participation they represent.

As another example may be mentioned the numerous international commodity agreements. Thus the constitution of the Cocoa Producers Alliance of 24 March 1970 provides in art. 8(1) that 200 out of the 1000 votes shall be equally distributed among the member states and that the remaining 800 votes shall be distributed in proportion to "the highest annual production of cocoa by each member" during the six preceding years.

In the Council of the European Communities those decisions which require a qualified majority are taken by weighted voting according to an arbitrary scale. Thus art. 148 of the EC Treaty allocates 10 votes to the big countries and from 2 to 8 to the others.

In most of these cases the decisions taken by weighted voting do not involve the exercise of powers over or within the member states, but merely exercise of powers over the important sums contributed by member states to the capital and the budget of the organization. However, in the European community, the provisions on weighted voting were a necessary tool in order to make the bigger countries agree to conferring upon the Community the power to make decisions binding upon and within the several member states.

If a system of weighted voting were introduced in the Security Council, it might be possible to mitigate or eliminate the veto power for certain members, which in turn would enable the Security Council to make more use of the powers of binding decision that it has under the Charter. If introduced in the General Assembly or in other international organizations, a system of weighted voting might enable the big powers to agree to accord to that organ or those organizations a power of making decisions binding upon its member states.

The next question is, what such powers could and should be conferred upon the UN or specialized international organizations? While the final aim should be a world federal government, one must start realistically in rather limited fields, where the need and the possibilities are greatest. These fields may be functional or geographical. I shall give a few brief examples of each.

Limited functional powers

With the rapid increase in population, industrialization, communications and pollution that the world has seen in this century, it is obvious that the need is increasing in several fields for international authorities which can make binding decisions within limited functional fields, not merely over means which the member states have contributed and placed at the disposal of the organization, like several of the organizations mentioned above, but even over the member states themselves and their territories and nationals.

This is particularly true within the field of protection of the environment in the broad sense. If recommendations by the United Nations and other global or regional organizations do not suffice, it will be necessary to confer upon such organizations the power to make binding decisions within certain limits by a qualified majority vote.

We have for several decades had the International Whaling Commission and regional fisheries commissions, whose purpose under their constitutions is to establish limitations upon the catch of fish and other maritime species in order to preserve the stock. So far the binding decisions of these commissions have been subject to a right of reservation, which implies a right for any member to declare itself not bound by the decision, while letting it enter into force for the others. It was the failure of these commissions – precisely because of the right of reservation – which provided the substantive justification for the vast expansion of national territorial waters and fisheries economic zones over the last decades, thus conferring a right upon the coastal state to issue regulations with binding effect for all. However, even with these expansions, there are still parts of the high seas which are not subject to the unilateral jurisdiction of a coastal state – quite apart from the fact that the effect of the unilateral regulation by one state in its economic zone may be nullified by the lack of regulations by other states of the same stock in their zones. An international power of binding decisions without a right of unilateral reservation may therefore still be necessary to conserve stocks. But it is not likely that states will be willing to abandon their right of reservation against such decisions unless the more important fisheries countries obtain a greater vote than the minor fisheries countries.

Also for the protection of the environment against pollution from industry and other sources, the world is probably now reaching a stage where more radical action has become necessary than can be achieved by voluntary co-operation between states with a right of veto or reservation.

Limited Geographic Areas:

International River Commissions

We already have some examples of international organizations which exercise limited functional powers in specific geographic areas, viz. the international river commissions. Indeed, the oldest international organization in the world is the Central Commission for Navigation on the Rhine, which was established in 1807 and which is still active. Another well-known example was the European Danube Commission, which was established in 1856 and continued in operation until the Second World War. Several such international river commissions have exercised binding legislative, administrative, judicial and fiscal powers in respect of navigation on the rivers concerned vis-á-vis ships of both member and non-member states. The riparian states in fact ceded to the organization their sovereign authority within the limited territory and the limited functional fields concerned. And most of these commissions exercise that authority by decisions made by weighted voting (directly or in disguised form).

There may arise a need for a similar delegation of authority to specialized international organizations for other functional fields in respect of international rivers – e.g. pollution – or for other geographic areas, such as national maritime zones (in connection with the high seas).

In territory not under national sovereignty one could even establish a general authority for the UN or for special international organizations. The most important example would be the high seas.

The High Seas

As far as the bottom of the high seas is concerned, an international regime was established by the Law of the Sea Convention of 1982. It established, in Part XI, rules for the international sea bed beyond the limits of national jurisdiction – called the "Area" – and an International Sea Bed Authority to administer that Area. The convention established *inter alia* the following principles for the Area:

Article 136
Common heritage of mankind
The Area and its resources are the common heritage of mankind.

Article 137
Legal status of the Area and its resources
1. No State shall claim or exercise sovereignty or sovereign rights, over any part of the Area or its resources, nor shall any State or natural or juridical person appropriate any part thereof. No such claim or exercise of sovereignty or sovereign rights nor such appropriation shall be recognized.

2. All rights in the resources of the area are vested in mankind as a whole, on whose behalf the Authority shall act. These resources are not subject to alienation. The minerals recovered from the Area, however, may only be alienated in accordance with this Pact and the rules, regulations and procedures of the Authority.

3. No State or natural or juridical person shall claim, acquire or exercise rights with respect to the minerals recovered from the Area except in accordance with this Pact. Otherwise, no such claim, acquisition or exercise of such rights shall be recognized.

The convention has so far been ratified by 51 states (by the end of 1991) and it will enter into force one year after it has been ratified by 60 states. From that time the International Sea Bed Authority will have legislative authority with regard to prospecting, exploration and exploitation of mineral resources in the Area. Indeed, the Authority will act as a territorial sovereign in respect of mineral resources at or beneath the sea-bed.

There are no direct provisions on weighted voting, but a disguised form of this is implied in the rules on the composition of the Council in art. 161(1).

The Authority or the UN or a specialized organization could also assume power over the international sea-bed in other functional fields, or even a general power over the sea-bed (as proposed by Malta), or even powers with regard to the high seas above. This they could do by additional conventions or by unilateral occupation. An occupation would extend the effect of the Authority's decisions to apply also *vis-á-vis* states which do not accede to the Law of the Sea Convention. A general occupation by the Authority, by the UN or by a special international organization would establish for that organization legislative, administrative and judicial powers also in other functional fields over the bottom of the sea and even over the high seas above.

Outer Space

Also with regard to outer space we already have several international treaties. However, they do not as yet establish an international authority – only principles and rules. The treaty of 25

January 1967 on Principles Governing the Activities of States in the Exploration and Use of Outer Space provides in art. 2:

Outer space, including the Moon and other celestial bodies, is not subject to national appropriation by claim of sovereignty, by means of use or occupation, or by any other means.

This provision precludes "national" occupation, but that does not preclude international occupation by the UN or a specialized international organization. Such occupation would enable the organization to establish further rules with jurisdiction over all states, whether or not they are parties to the 1967 treaty. Politically it would of course be necessary first to negotiate the terms of an international regime for outer space. But a formal occupation would prevent such a regime from being stopped or disobeyed by a minority of states, as it would give the regime legal effect vis-á-vis all states.

Antarctica

The position of Antarctica differs from that of the high seas and outer space in two respects:

1. Seven states have claimed sectors in Antarctica. There is only one sector which has not been claimed (Eastern Pacific). These claims, however, have not been recognized by the non-claimant parties to the Antarctic Treaty. Moreover, there are no fewer than three states claiming the same and most important sector (The Graham Peninsula south of South America).

2. Like the international river treaties, the Antarctic Treaty has established an international organization composed of the claimant states and other contracting states which are active in the area.

If agreement can be reached between the parties to the treaty, the Antarctic Treaty Organization could occupy Antarctica and thereby assume territorial legislative, administrative and judicial authority over the land territory and the maritime zones with effect vis-á-vis all states. This regime could then include also the unclaimed sector. In this manner one could establish one common regime for all parts of Antarctica. There would be more likelihood of the claimant states being willing to yield their claims to the Antarctic Treaty Organization than to the UN and this would also be the most practical solution.

Has an international organization legal "power" to occupy territory?

International lawyers will automatically raise the question as to whether the United Nations or the Antarctic Treaty Organization or any other international organization has the legal "power" to occupy such territories. Many would look to the constitution of the organization concerned for authority to do this – and find none without resorting to a very fanciful interpretation.

However, this is not at all necessary. First it should be pointed out that the resort to the constitution of the organization is based partly upon a false analogy to the internal law of certain countries, which do not recognize associations and companies as legal persons of their own, except in those cases and to the extent that this has been laid down by statute. This analogy disregards the basic difference that there is no legislative authority in international law.

In the second place, there has been a failure to distinguish between the legal capacity of international organizations and other self-governing communities to perform acts of international law in the same manner as other subjects of international law – i.e. on the basis of equality – and their power (i.e. authority) to make decisions binding upon other subjects of international law. (The two are in legal doctrine frequently confused under the still popular term of "implied powers", meaning powers which one attempts to interpret into a constitution which never was intended to define or delimit international legal capacity.)

The latter requires clear legal basis, implying consent from the states concerned (delegated power); a fanciful interpretation of the constitution of the organization concerned will not normally suffice to that effect. On the other hand, the consent need not be embodied in the constitution at all — it may be founded in any other treaty or in a unilateral act by the state or states concerned or in customary law.

The former, however, requires no specific legal basis, as it is founded in general international law. International organizations — like states and other self-governing communities — have an inherent legal capacity to perform international acts which do not impose new obligations upon states or other legal subjects. This is firmly established in international customary law and now also recognized by the International Court of Justice in its advisory opinion of 20 July 1962 on Certain Expenses of the United Nations (ICJ Reports 1962, p. 168). The condition is merely that the act is not precluded by provisions of their constitutions or by other treaties or rules of international law. Thus, an occupation requires no relevant provision in the constitution of the organization concerned (or in any other treaty) as long as it falls within the limits of the purposes stated in the constitution (as it does both in the case of the UN and the Antarctic Treaty Organization) and as long as the constitution contains no other provision precluding it (as it normally does not) and as long as it does not violate general international law.

Thus from a legal point of view no charter amendment or other treaty provision is required to enable the organizations concerned to occupy unilaterally such territory as is not already subject to national sovereignty. This covers the high seas, the international sea-bed, outer space, celestial bodies and the unclaimed sector in Antarctica. Here the occupation is merely one of legal capacity, which international organizations have.

However, this capacity is not sufficient to give the organization the right to occupy territory which is already subject to national jurisdiction, such as international rivers or the claimed sectors in Antarctica to the extent that the claims are considered internationally valid. Neither the UN, nor any other international organization, can, any more than a state, acquire powers in a national territory without the consent of the state concerned. Nor can the UN or an international fisheries commission or any other organization unilaterally assume the power to make decisions binding upon states in functional fields. But even this does not require any revision of the UN Charter or of the constitution of the other international organizations concerned. It is enough that the states concerned agree by separate treaty or unilateral act to confer the power upon the organization.

On the other hand, a revision of the charter or the constitution of the other organization concerned is required in order to introduce weighted voting, because the present constitutions of the UN (arts. 18 and 27) and of most other organizations now provide that each member shall have one vote.

A world federation?

If we succeed in establishing some of these or other powers for the UN and certain specialized international organizations, and we see that they work, then states may prove willing to continue along this road and establish genuine powers for the UN and other international organizations in further fields more directly relevant to peace and security. Such a gradual development towards a democratic world federation with its own armed force may provide the guarantee for world peace that we need. This must be our long term goal. Modern constitutions of some states already foresee this possibility. Thus art. 24 of the constitution (Grundgesetz) of the German Federal Republic provides *inter alia* that "*Der Bund kann durch Gesetz Hoheitsrechte auf zwischenstaatliche Einrichtungen übertragen*" (the Federation can through legislation transfer sovereignty rights to international institutions.)

Subsidiarity

HANNA NEWCOMBE*

Political ideologies can be dichotomized in various ways. One of the most important in our time is "centralization" and "decentralization". People who want to plan the economy on a grand scale, or build large power nets for energy distribution, or trade with distant parts of the world, are "centralizers". These might include both communists or socialists (who extol planning) and liberals (who believe in worldwide free trade regardless of local inequities this might produce). On the other hand, those (like the Greens) who believe in the use of local resources, growing your own food, generating electric power at a local level, and building community from the bottom up, are the decentralizers.

It might seem obvious to class World Federalists among the centralizers. Aren't they always talking about "global problems" and "global solutions"? Don't they want to switch our allegiance from our nation to the world? Don't they want a world government to override national decisions, at least in the field of armaments, war and pollution?

Yet we should not think of World Federalists as centralizers, necessarily. Let us think of them, rather, as centralizers and decentralizers at the same time. What needs to be done is to de-emphasize the national level of decision-making, which has become the subject of intense idolatrous worship in the last few centuries (under the name of "nationalism"), and drain power from this national level in two directions: downward to the peo-

---

* A shorter version was published by Canadian World Federalist.

ple, the individual persons at the grass roots, and upward to the whole of humanity everywhere, in fact to the whole living Earth.

"From Person to Person" would be a fitting description of this aspiration.

World Federalists are problem-oriented and problem-specific: they would centralize decisions on such matters as universal disarmament and global reforestation, where the effects of wrong-headed policies would have worldwide effects, beyond any boundary lines we care to draw on a map. They would insist that the basic source of "sovereignty", i.e. decision-making power, is the individual citizen, who can delegate this power to any level of government that seems most suitable; this is just basic democratic theory, and we abide by this.

Yes, it is true, of course, that "global problems require global solutions". But what about local problems? Would they not require local solutions, and should we not insist on higher levels of government not interfering? An example might be the local generation of electricity from a small local stream that falls over the escarpment, like Websters Falls in Dundas. The amount of electric power generated would be small, and some engineers sneer at it; but if every community did this, and became locally self-reliant, the national energy needs could come closer to being met. The motto might be to utilize every drop that falls over any cliff.

Another example of localization being the better solution is food. Everyone prefers vegetables fresh from one's own garden; they taste better and are more nutritious. Long-distance transport of food leads to partial spoilage, or requires expensive refrigeration, or leads to the use of preservative technologies like freezing, drying or canning (or, Heaven help us, irradiation), all of which degrade food value to some extent. Better to eat local produce and eat according to season ("pig out on strawberries in June" as someone has said).

Yet we must not over-romanticize our "green-ness". Worldwide trade in many commodities and manufactures is still to the mutual advantage of both partners in many cases, especially when mineral resources are concerned: tin in Bolivia, copper in

Chile or Zaire, oil in Saudi Arabia, etc. Specialization in manufacturing may also be advantageous, so that in one locality people might get very good at making textiles, in another place steel, and in yet another place computers. These things don't spoil in long-range transport (though transport adds to their cost), and mutual exchange may enhance international friendships as well as give economic advantages. Yet caution is required, since totally free trade (purely by market mechanisms) may lead to exploitation of some countries by others. A judicious mix of planning and market methods would probably be best at the world level as well as at national levels; but these are just two different ways of managing centralization, which is our main topic here.

It is time then to state the guiding principle of centralization-decentralization. This is called *The Principle of Subsidiarity*, and is of ancient origin. It states: "Problems should be solved at the lowest level consistent with efficient performance of the task." Or alternatively, "Problems should be solved at the lowest level possible at which there are no significant external effects."

The presumption is to the lowest level possible, because it is closer to the people, the ultimate unit of democratic responsibility. The terms "efficient performance" and "significant external effects" somewhat beg the question, and need some additional comment. However, they will always remain somewhat vague, a matter of judgement; this is the root of the jurisdictional disputes in all federations (e.g. between provincial and federal domains), with which we are very familiar in Canada.

Nevertheless, let us try to be a bit more specific. What do we mean by "external effects"? Suppose that a town decides to discharge its sewage into the river. There will obviously be external effects outside the town's boundaries, especially to all the towns downstream on the same river. Therefore the town should not have the sovereign right to do with its sewage as it pleases. The regulation must come from higher levels, perhaps provincial, that encompasses the whole river valley (or the Greens' notion of a "bio-region" might be applied.) But if the town decides to have a by-law prohibiting noise in the streets after midnight, that is truly its own business, because it does not affect anyone outside the town. The principle is really the same as that stated by John Stuart Mill of individuals: a person has complete freedom to exercise one's rights, as long as the exercise of those rights does not interfere with the rights of others. The same applies to towns and to nations.

So, jumping to the other end, which would be the truly global problems requiring a world government? Obviously, the problem of war: even a local war may escalate, and even a limited nuclear exchange can produce "nuclear winter" which might kill everyone on earth. We should include not only war itself, but also armaments, both because of the danger to peace which they pose, and because of the expense, which impoverishes everyone, especially the already poor. Also among global problems are some of the larger environmental problems: damage to the ozone layer, global warming, deforestation, desertification, ocean pollution and acid rain (which obviously crosses national borders). However, some environmental problems, like the river pollution cited earlier, may be more local in scope. The problem of a economic inequality among nations (problems of "development") is also global because it affects the stability of peace, and also because a purely national solution of the problem is not possible in many cases (e.g. in small landlocked nations in Africa). Yet self-reliance should be promoted whenever and wherever possible.

The problem of human rights violations is still in dispute as to its global or national nature. In the UN there is a constant argument going on between two articles of the Charter, the one about safeguarding human rights and the one about preserving national sovereignty. Large-scale violations which lead to an outflow of refugees spill over into neighbouring countries and become global, or at least regional problems. But even in other cases, feelings of human solidarity are now strong enough that we would want to give some help to our suffering brothers and sisters under tyrannical regimes. Yet intervention (especially armed intervention) is a very serious danger to peace. This remains a borderline case in the subsidiarity debate, and a very vexatious one. Obviously we do not have a complete theory of subsidiarity that would answer all questions in an unambiguous manner.

Elsewhere (*Peace Actions at the Municipal Level*, Peace Research Reviews, Vol. XI, No. 2, Sept. 1988) we have outlined the 6 levels (individual, neighbourhood, town, metropolis or province, nation, world) of government that might be needed in a "multi-level world". If 100 individuals aggregate into a neighbourhood, 100 neighbourhoods into a town (10,000 people), 100 towns into a metropolis or province (1 million people), 10 metro regions into a (large) nation (100 million people), and 100 nations into the world (10 billion people – we are not quite there yet), it would take only 6 steps to go from Person to Planet.

Some of these levels of governments already exist, but some do not. Let us go out and create both neighbourhood governments and a world government: repair both the bottom and the top of our world to make it complete and whole.

Reform of the UN Security Council

HANNA NEWCOMBE*

It has been suggested that the UN Security Council, which has recently come into prominence because of its vigorous action (this term does not indicate approval) in the Gulf crisis, should be strengthened for further actions (hopefully more preventive in nature) that may be needed, in this or other future crises. Since great-power unanimity has now been achieved, many people rejoice that "the UN is now operating as its founders intended". However, present consensus among the Big Five is not necessarily permanent, nor will it remain applicable to future situations. This may be the appropriate time for reform, when conditions are plastic and so many other things are changing in international relations.

What reforms should be recommended? In 1979, I prepared a comprehensive review of proposals for Security Council Reform. (Peace Research Reviews, Vol. VIII, No. 3, May 1979, 104 pp.) Perusing that volume now, I will try to pick out what might be applicable to the circumstances of today.

The number of Permanent Members should probably be increased, just to reflect the reality of newly rising world powers (economic powers, not just military). To the present Big Five (US, USSR, UK, France and China) should be added Japan and united Germany – the former "enemy nations" of World War II. Paying some regard also to the high-population countries in the Third World that certainly carry weight in the international system, the inclusion of India, Brazil and Nigeria have been suggested, to represent the three continents of Asia, South

---

* Reprinted from Canadian World Federalist, March 1991.

America, and Africa in the south. This would result in 10 permanent members; however, this may be too many, since the difficulty of reaching consensus increases with the number of permanent members. One suggestion for remedying this problem is to combine UK, France and Germany into one permanent seat for the EC, which may soon have a unified foreign policy. This would make 8 permanent members, perhaps still too many.

One way out would be to modify or soften the veto, in a supplementary reform. This can be done by any of the following ways: (a) Restricting the veto to fewer nations, perhaps only to the two superpowers. (Being a Permanent Member of the Security Council would be separate from having a veto.) (b) Imposing a quota of only so many vetos permitted per year for each veto power. (c) Requiring 2 or more negative votes by veto powers to constitute a veto, not only one as at present. (d) Substituting qualified majorities of the whole 15-member Security Council for the veto. (Thus, if one-third was required to block a decision, a member attempting to exercise veto power would have to find at least 4 other negative votes among the 7 permanent or 7 non-permanent members.) (e) Using bicameral arrangements with the General Assembly, e.g. the right to over-rule a Security Council veto by a 4/5 majority in the General Assembly. (f) Limiting the application of the veto to certain classes of issues. (Excluding e.g. membership applications and conflict resolution.)

This represents a wide menu of choices for Security Council Reform. In conclusion, let us choose one possibility for a closer look. Let us assume that we have a Security Council composed of 8 permanent members (US, USSR, EC, China, Japan, India, Brazil, Nigeria), with only 2 (US and USSR) having the veto, plus 7 non-permanent members elected (as at present) by the General Assembly on a regional basis. Secondly, let us modify the voting rules as in (a) and (d) above. If the US and the USSR both vote against a resolution, it will be considered vetoed. If, say, only the US votes against, it might (or might not) be able to find allies in EC and Japan among the veto-less permanent members, plus two more allies among the non-permanent members (which may be possible, because 2 of the non-permanent members traditionally come from a group called Western Europe and Other). But US allies do not always agree with US politics, so the outcome would not be certain. Similarly, if the USSR votes against, they might find allies among Third World nations (both permanent and non-permanent members), but they might not. The rule would be that unless at least one veto-power (US or USSR) plus 4 other Security Council members (to constitute 5 out of 15, i.e. a one-third blocking group) vote against a resolution, it will pass, in spite of the veto.

Such a changed composition of the Security Council in combination with a change in the voting rules might strengthen the Security Council by making it more representative of the world of the 1990s and at the same time more able to act decisively in crisis situations.

Toward Global Perestroika: Domesticating Technology

ROBERT BETCHOV

The most obvious difference between humans and animals is changing technology. While bees know how to build bee-hives and birds can construct various kinds of nests, their technology does not evolve through the ages. In contrast, the human ability to use brain and hands has developed very slowly during our long prehistory, and gradually gained speed. Today, as we approach the twenty-first century, we are confronted by a formidable range of opportunities and perils.

Humankind has reached a point where technology must be domesticated. This is a worldwide problem that cannot be handled within each human tribe. It is a planetary challenge that 200 independent governments may not even be able to master.

Throughout history, technological innovations have brought various social changes and the speed of cultural evolution has triggered revolutions in laws as well as in mental attitudes.

Today, at the end of the XXth century, technology is raising great hopes of economic improvements as well as formidable threats of atomic destruction or chemical pollution. The purpose of the present paper is to review the past, survey the present and take a glimpse at the future. Essentially , we intend to show that we must domesticate technology and that this calls for a limitation of national sovereignty.

Before 1800

In times long ago, I imagine our ancestors living in caves and eating fruits and raw meat. Then, after a forest fire or a volcanic eruption, some bright individuals discovered how to keep a few flames alive between three large stones, and with a provision of fire-wood. This brought daily meals of fried meat, greater comfort during cold nights and the first quiet fire-side chats.

The fire-place then moved inside the cave. Since matches were not available some folks got the task of keeping the flame alive, day or night. They also prevented children from tossing burning branches into the fire, simply to enjoy the first fireworks. Thus, with the conquest of fire, the human collectivity had to modify its social structure and to make new rules.

Many other advances followed, but we shall make a huge leap over the centuries and millennia, as is necessary in this brief survey.

In ancient China, the idea of a device able to print characters had been used. The first European printing press built by Gutenberg in Strasbourg must have appeared as an innocent machine. Soon after, translated versions of the Bible came into many hands, and partly as a result of this, the Christian world became divided between Catholics opposed to such a spread of ideas and those who favoured the change.

The printing press stimulated literacy. Those who read the Bible for themselves, rather than having it interpreted by the priest, became the leaders and followers of the Reformation. The small city of Geneva became the center of a new society. Between its high walls, it attracted the adherents of a particular stream of the Reformation; they came from Hungary, Scotland, and elsewhere. Calvin became the great master of the new ideology, ruling the city with an iron hand. After his death the citizens decided to "de-Calvinize" (as we might now say). This early example of *perestroika* and *glasnost* opened the door to religious tolerance an the concept of freedom of the press.

Another Geneva citizen, Jean Jacques Rousseau, who was mainly active in France before the French Revolution, pleaded for the general education of all children and the adoption of a printed set of laws. He stood for public schools and the social contract.

Long before, there had already been written legal codes, for example, Roman law and Islamic law. The Vikings and the Swiss mountaineers had developed their own traditions to settle the problems encountered by fishermen or Alpine farmers. A *Tingr* or a *Landsgemeinde* was an annual meeting of the male citizens, voting by raising hands and directly electing their leaders. In Runic characters, the Norsemen wrote their principle: "The land must be ruled by law and not wasted by war". In Gothic letters, the men of Uri, Schwyz and Unterwald concluded a pact where we read: "If a conflict occurs among us, we will bring it to the wisest judges, and anyone not abiding by their decision shall be our common enemy".

In England, from the Magna Carta to the first constitutional monarchy, we see the development of a parliamentary system in which the prime minister has to deal with *His/Her Majesty's Loyal Opposition.*

In the New World, the Virginians and the other colonists rebelled against their British rulers, obtained their independence, and a few years later wrote the American Constitution. The Senate represented the various states, from Boston puritans to Alabama slave holders. The House of Representatives operated on the principle of One-Person-One-Vote (at first only men, later including women).

Soon after, the king of France, faced with an archaic social and financial system, called for a meeting of a set of three separate assemblies for Church, Nobility and the Third Estate. After Church and Nobility refused to join in a single constitutional assembly, the citizens rebelled and the king lost his head, as did the queen and most of the members of the aristocracy.

Thus, within four hundred years, from Gutenberg to Guillotin, technology together with political ideology and religion, brought profound social changes.

The XIXth Century

With the XIXth Century came the steam engine, electric telegraph and the first flying machines. Less spectacular, but essential were the discoveries of Nobel (dynamite) and Pasteur (the role of bacteria in many processes, beneficial or harmful). Within three generations, the railroad and the steamboat brought nations together. With dynamite, the engineers could rely on a safe but powerful explosive. It became possible to dig tunnels under the Alps and to open sea lanes such as the canals of Suez and Panama. However, in military applications, new kinds of cartridges allowed the invention of machine guns. Thus cavalry became obsolete. The battle of Tshushima between Japanese and Russian fleets demonstrated that technology knows no ethnic boundaries.

Technological progress was increasingly aided by mathematics; for engineering purposes the Arabic numerals — which so facilitate arithmetical operations — had become universally accepted, relegating Roman numerals to the faces of clocks and to chapter headings.

Before Pasteur, all attempts to feed animal milk to infants had met with trouble. One old legend told of a young god able to survive on a diet of goat's milk. Our ancestors may not have known about germs, but at least they knew about contagious diseases. In times of war, the bodies of victims of plague or cholera had been catapulted into besieged cities to start epidemics.

After Pasteur's discoveries, humanity won a major victory over disease. Physicians and midwives learned to scrub their hands and wear rubber gloves. This technology greatly reduced infant and maternal mortality. When a mother could not give enough milk, it was no longer necessary to hire a nurse. Pasteurized milk could help. Pasteur invented vaccination against rabies. It soon extended to many other diseases. Today, from Geneva, the World Health Organization sees to it that a vaccine against varicella or typhus injected in Singapore is equally effective in Sweden or Mexico, against all known forms of the illness.

A woman no longer has to go through ten pregnancies and nursing periods in order to have two adolescent children. Her own average life span nearly doubled.

Electricity was a new field. In 1890, Branly used a magnetic powder to detect the reception of radio waves. Messages could now travel faster than the horseman or any system of waving flags. The planet started to shrink.

In the last decade of the 19th century, in a lonely Russian *isba* (room), a hard-of-hearing man realized what new changes chemistry could allow. Konstantin Tsiolkowsky is the father of the space age. Around 1883, he explained what rocket engines could do. Writing with a goose feather, he calculated without the help of electronic machines, the mass of fuel necessary to take one man to the Moon on a single vehicle. He showed that the empty fuel tanks and initial engines should be dropped as dead weight. Should we use two, three, ten or a hundred successive rocket stages? Today, our students learn to program his formula on a computer. It shows what Tsiolkowsky found by hand and mailed to a Moscow publisher: three stages are sufficient for most missions.

Tsiolkowsky was not only a brilliant engineer. He clearly perceived that technology would profoundly alter human life and call for new political institutions. Before the 1917 Russian revolution, in his visionary essay entitled *Outside the Earth*, we read:

"What was our Earth like in the year 2017, to which our narrative relates?:

"There was a single authority for the whole world, a congress of elected representatives of all nations. It had been inaugurated more than 70 years before, and it dealt with all of mankind's problems. Wars were impossible. Misunderstanding between peoples were settled by peaceful means. Armies were drastically limited, or rather they were labour armies. Thanks to the fairly favourable conditions of the preceding one hundred years, the population had trebled."

Another pioneer was Ader. A practical man, he was fascinated by the idea of building a flying machine. This is not a problem that can be studied with a goose feather or even a supercomputer. The engineer can use wind tunnels, but the final proof comes on the airfield. Ader built his first airplane and took off the ground in 1890.

The idea of international law had progressed. The Red Cross Conventions of 1868 had been signed and successfully applied. A dispute between the US and Great Britain, at the time of the American Civil War, stemming from the case of the Alabama ship, had been settled before an arbitration tribunal in Geneva. An International Parliamentary Union was founded in Paris in 1888. In 1899, a comprehensive peace conference opened in The Hague. The ambassadors unanimously condemned the launching of projectiles from balloons, but failed to forbid unanimously the dum-dum bullet. At the turn of the century the International Court of Arbitration was ready to start operating. It remained largely unused, but became the starting point of the International Court of Justice operating today.

The XXth Century

The first decade saw rapid progress in aviation and radio telegraphy. In Berne, a young physicist employed by the Patent Office, Albert Einstein, was spending his free time pondering his new hypothesis that the speed of light is unaffected by the velocity of the observer. His theory of relativity would soon win for him a professorship in Berlin.

In Sarajevo, in August 1914, a terrorist triggered the first world war.

In Berlin, a senior professor of surgery wrote an appeal to the German Emperor Wilhelm II. The war could only bring ruin to all parties: the best outcome would be a negotiated settlement. In the entire university, he found only a single co-signer: the recently appointed Albert Einstein.

The war revealed that machine gun and heavy artillery would dominate the battle field. Poison gas was extensively used for the first time. The conflict ended with the collapse of the empires of Germany, Austria, Russia and Turkey.

When peace came, the soldiers returning from the trenches and the women liberated from work in the ammunition factories turned for hope towards US President Wilson. He promised collective security and general and complete disarmament under a new League of Nations. But the American senators opposed US membership in the League of Nations, created in Geneva. The Covenant of the League started with the words: *"The High Contracting Parties . . ."* and important decisions required unanimity. Thus, every member nation had a veto in the League's Council.

In 1946, after the atomic bombing of Hiroshima, when the League met for its last session, the last speaker concluded with the words:

" It is not the League that failed the nations. It is the nations that failed the League. The League is dead, long live the United Nations."

Einstein's relativity theory had given an unexpected result: the energy E of an object at rest is given by the formula mc^2, where m is the mass and c is the velocity of light in a vacuum. The loss of mass in nuclear reactions could now explain the heat from volcanos and the energy from hydrogen that keeps the sun shining bright, as well as the energy released in nuclear fission.

After Hitler 's invasion of Poland in 1939, the second world war started and Einstein drew the attention of President Roosevelt to the possibility of building atom bombs.

Between the two wars, Einstein had discussed the question of peace. In a booklet *Why War?* published jointly with Sigmund Freud in 1932, he asked for the means to free mankind from the threat of war. He stated:

"For me, an individual free from national prejudices, the external face of the problem – the matter of organization – appears simple. The nations must create a legislative and judicial organization for the settlement of all conflicts that can arise among them. They must pledge to submit to the laws made by the legislative branch, to bring all disputes before the courts, to abide without reservations to its decisions in order to assure application, and to carry out any measures deemed necessary by the court".

Further down, we read:

"The path leading to international security requires that the Member States abandon without conditions a part of their freedom of action, in other words, of their sovereignty. There is no doubt that no other path to security can be found".

In his reply Freud stresses that the notion of law cannot be separated from that of force, or more clearly, of violence. Might and Right are not opposite, but complementary.

As the second World War approached the end, the diplomats met in San Francisco to draft a new social contract: the United Nations Charter. But they had no idea what was brewing in secret laboratories: atom bombs and intercontinental ballistic missiles.

The UN Charter starts with the words: "We the People of the United Nations . . .", but its next Article declares that the UN is based on the principle of equal sovereignty of the member nations. Furthermore, five nations got special (permanent) seats in the Security Council with the right of veto. Each nation has one vote in the General Assembly. Historians tell that, in the Yalta Conference, Stalin wanted one seat for each of the fifteen Soviet republics. Truman replied that, in that case, the US should join as 48 states. A compromise was reached: the three most populous Soviet republics joined as sovereign nations. Thus, in the UN and every international organization patterned after it, the flags of Russia, Ukraine, and Byelorussia fly from the roof on opening days, next to the US flag, among some 150 flags of other nation-states.

In 1990 Byelorussia came in fifth place down the list of Soviet populations, after Uzbekhistan and Kazakhstan. Should some flags be changed? [Undoubtedly, they will be after the demise of the Soviet Union at the end of 1991 (editor's note).]

After the atomic bombing of Hiroshima, some journalists visited Einstein and asked for his opinion. He replied that the atom bomb means that we need a world government. The surprised visitors asked what kind of world government, and Einstein advised them to read a book recently published by his friend Emery Reves entitled *The Anatomy of Peace*.

In Geneva, Emery Reves directed a press bureau during the life of the League of Nations. Even before the atom bomb, he felt that the UN Charter would fail to provide planetary security. He envisioned a world federal authority with a parliament based on rationality, and empowered to make laws binding on the individual citizen of the member nations.

In the spring of 1945 Emery Reves wrote:

"It is natural that in any universal organization created today, representation should be determined by actual responsibilities and according to effective power, industrial potential, degree of education. Various proved methods exist and can be applied to work out this purely technical question."

In 1955, two American law experts, Grenville Clark and Louis B. Sohn, proposed a major revision of the UN Charter in their book *World Peace Through World Law*. At this time, the only available data on the state of the planet consisted of tables giving for each nation the geographic area and the population. Figures on Gross National Product were incomplete and controversial. Clark and Sohn proposed a quantized system for voting in the new UN General Assembly: the first four nations down the table of populations get 30 seats each, the next 15 get 8 seats each, and so forth down to a minimum of one seat for the smallest nations.

The reader interested in this "technical question" will find a broad survey in *Design for a Better World*, by Hanna Newcombe (University Press of America, Lanham, M.D. (1983)).

After the uranium bomb came the hydrogen (H) bomb. The Hiroshima fire ball was about one kilometer tall. The very first H bomb produced a fireball ten times larger, reaching the upper limit of the atmosphere. It produced an unexpected electro-magnetic pulse (EMP) far from the site of the explosion. Washington and Moscow wisely decided to stop any such tests in the atmosphere or in outer space. [But only after widespread popular protest (editor's note).] Thus, on both sides of the iron curtain, the EMP became a menace hanging over all electrical devices, computers, and means of communication, just as the bombs themselves were deadly threats to all the people.

After the launching of the first Sputnik in 1957, it was clear that the United States no longer led the world technologically in lonely isolation, and the Soviets gained confidence from their ability to take the lead in a special space project.

The first American H bomb was designed by Edward Teller. But his device was far too bulky to be transported by airplane or ship. In the USSR, Andrei Sakharov proceeded along a different idea and his H bomb was the first real military device. From his very first declaration, Sakharov stressed the danger of this technology and the need for a new social contract. In Washington and in Moscow, the political leaders took note of the physicists' warnings, but failed to initiate any major political changes. They accepted a balance of terror, with H bombs placed on missiles aboard nuclear submarines or in underground silos. Los Angeles lived under the threat from Siberia and Leningrad from Oklahoma.

With the development of various space rockets, each super-power looked at the possibility of anti-ballistic-missiles (ABMs). If we see an enemy missile approaching one of our large cities with a ten megaton bomb, what can we do? Some engineers proposed to build radar-directed ABMs aimed at the incoming weapon. A small plutonium bomb would destroy the target. Other scientists pointed out that the attacking missiles could be surrounded with much lighter rockets, just to confuse the defense. Such decoys could be cheap and effective.

In 1972 Washington and Moscow agreed to build not more than 100 ABMs on each side. This prevented a wasteful escalation of technology. It also gives each party a way to react to any accidental or erroneous missile launching. The ABM Treaty is an example of domesticated technology.

In 1983 in Washington, a system of laser-equipped space satellites was proposed that was intended to keep the US safe from enemy attacks. This "Star Wars" project met with strong opposition, from citizens and members of the Congress and some scientists.

Now the Soviet *perestroika* brought the end of the balance of terror. [Nevertheless the Star Wars project just alluded to is continuing! (editors note).]

In 1989, the US and the USSR both won the Cold War by not fighting a hot war. The losers were the advocates of a return to Stalinism.

In Moscow, back from his exile in Gorky, Sakharov started to speak as the parliamentary leader of *His Majesty's Loyal Opposition*. The press gained considerable freedom.

Thus, in less than ten years, the USSR started to catch up with what others had experienced through the Reformation, the Thirty Years War, the American and French Revolutions. In Moscow and in every Soviet republic, the search for new social contracts has started.

The XXth Century saw the proliferation of international organizations. The World Health Organization and World Meteorological Organization have general assemblies patterned after the UN charter: One-Nation-One-Vote. In the World Bank, the votes reflect the financial power of the member nations. In the executive council of INMARSAT, which from London looks after communications by satellites between ships on the high seas and shore stations, the votes are in proportion to the duration of communications. These communications contribute not only to naval safety, but also to good fishing and meterological forecasting.

The attempt to promote a Law of the Sea to manage the seabed and protect the oceans from various sources of pollution became bogged down. The central question was weighted voting.

Any agreement on the ozone layer or verification of arms limitation will also run into the question of inspection and industrial monitoring. Thus as we come to the end our century, and review the advice of the people who made technology what it is, we must ask ourselves two basic questions:

1. Can we domesticate technology?
2. Can two hundred sovereign governments take effective steps?

This is the problem of global *perestroika*.

Weighted Voting at the United Nations

ROBERT BETCHOV

If the United Nations is to be strengthened in order to deal decisively with world problems, many observers feel that the voting system in the UN General Assembly will have to be revamped. Many schemes have been proposed, and 25 of them have been tested and compared by H. Newcombe (*Design for a Better World*, University Press of America, 1983).

This paper is a computer-assisted comparison of 11 such schemes. The voting weights are given in the diagrams on subsequent pages, not by nation for all (ca.) 160 nations, but by region, of which 9 are designated. The "regions" are actually political rather than geographic groupings.

It is readily seen that different weighted voting schemes favour different world regions. This will obviously influence the decision (if and when it comes) of which scheme will be chosen by world leaders.

Two of the diagrams represent the Soviet Union as 15 separate republics, an extension of the system in which the USSR has 3 votes in the UN – Russia, Ukraine and Byelorussia.

On January 22, 1992, the Tribune de Genéve published some figures on the net production per inhabitant of each of the fifteen former Soviet republics. Soviet manuals say that the USSR accounts for 20% of the world industrial production. This means 120 votes in an industrial-production-based assembly of 600 seats. The UN Energy Yearbook gives 118 votes in an energy-consumption-based assembly.

I took this net-production index to see how the seats of the former USSR would be distributed in an assembly of 600 seats, according to population, industry or half population and half industry. The results, rounded off to the nearest integer for fixed total votes according to population (column A), industrial production (column B) and half and half (column C) are tabulated in Table I.

Table I

	Population	Industry	Population and Industry
	A	B	C
Russia	17	72	45
Ukraine	6	19	13
Byelorussia	1	5	3
Lithuania	1	2	1
Latvia	0	1	1
Estonia	0	1	0
Moldavia	1	1	1
Georgia	1	2	1
Armenia	0	1	1
Azerbaijan	1	2	1
Kazakhstan	2	5	3
Nzbekistan	2	4	3
Tadjikistan	1	1	1
Kirghistan	1	1	1
Turkmenistan	0	1	1
TOTAL	34	118	76

Conclusions

The diagrams which follow show that, among the voting schemes:

- — "Flags" (one-nation-one-vote) favours Third World nations
- — "People" (vote proportional to population) favours China and Asia
- — "Tec" (vote proportional to energy consumption) favours the West and USSR
- — "$" (vote proportional to GNP) favours the West and Japan
- — "Student" (vote proportional to education expenditure) favours the West, Japan and USSR
- — "Nurse" (vote proportional to health expenditure) favours the West, Japan and USSR
- — "People and Tec" (population and energy consumption) favours most regions almost equally
- — "People and $" (population and GNP) favours most regions almost equally
- — "People and student" (population and Education expenditure) favours most regions almost equally
- — "People and nurse" (population and health expenditure) favours most regions almost equally
- — "Flags, people and tec" (nation, population and energy expenditure) favours China and the Third World

Thus, if we desire approximate political balance between the regions, the two-factor schemes would be the best choice. The same conclusion was reached in H. Newcombe's book cited above.

Which voting scheme would be chosen by the leaders of nations if they decided to adopt weighted voting would probably be decided by negotiations in which each leader would try to maximize the benefit to his/her own nation, and some compromise would be reached. Calculations such as these would act only as a guide to the political deliberations.

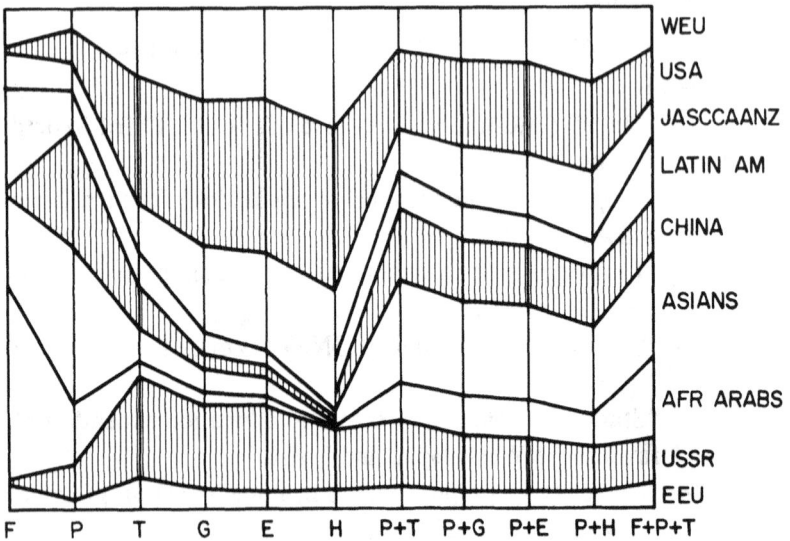

Eleven Weighted Voting Systems and Nine World Regions.

Each of the intervals in the diagrams shows how many seats would be allocated to nine regional groups of nations under one particular weighted voting rule.

WEU	Western European nations
USA	United States of America
JASCCANZ	Various developed nations such as Japan, four Scandinavians, Canada, Australia, New Zealand, etc.
LATIN AM	Latin America, from Mexico to Cape Horn
CHINA	Mainland China
ASIANS	Asia, less China, Japan and some Arab nations
AFR + ARAB	Africa and most Arab nations
USSR	Fifteen former Soviet republics
EEU	Eastern Europe

F	Flags: One-nation-one-vote (UN General Assembly)
P	Peoples: One-person-one-vote
T	Technological power, from UN energy consumption data: One-tec-one-vote
G	Gross National Product, in $ (Sivard data) (One-dollar-one-vote)
E	Size of Educational establishment (Sivard data) (One-student-one-vote)
H	Size of Health Care establishment (Sivard data) (One-nurse-one-vote)
P+T	Population and energy consumption, half and half
P+G	Population and GNP, half and half
P+E	Population and Education, half and half
P+H	Population and Health, half and half
F+P+T	One vote per nation, 200 by Population and 200 by tec.

Data: *UN 1987 Energy Statistics Yearbook* (1 tec = 1 ton equivalent coal); Sivard, Ruth *1986 World Military and Social Expenditures*, WMSE Publications.

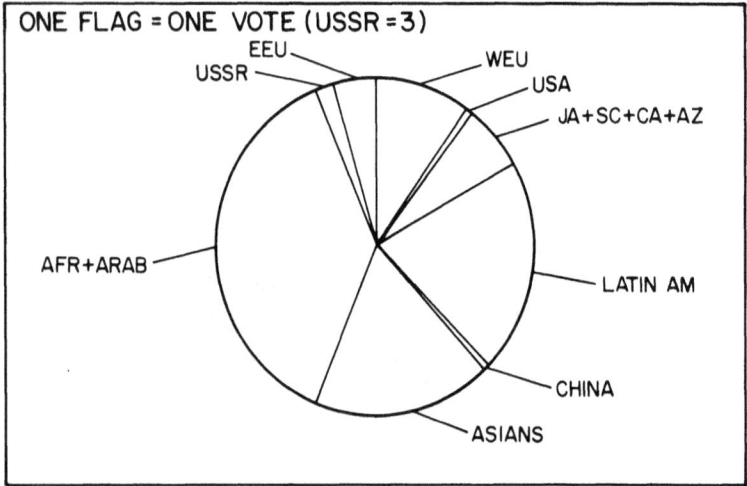

ONE FLAG = ONE VOTE (USSR = 3)

EEU
USSR
WEU
USA
JA+SC+CA+AZ
AFR+ARAB
LATIN AM
CHINA
ASIANS

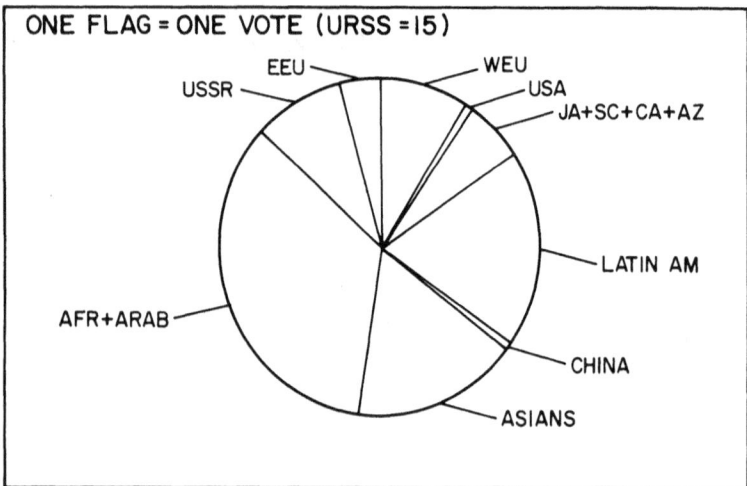

ONE FLAG = ONE VOTE (URSS = 15)

EEU
USSR
WEU
USA
JA+SC+CA+AZ
AFR+ARAB
LATIN AM
CHINA
ASIANS

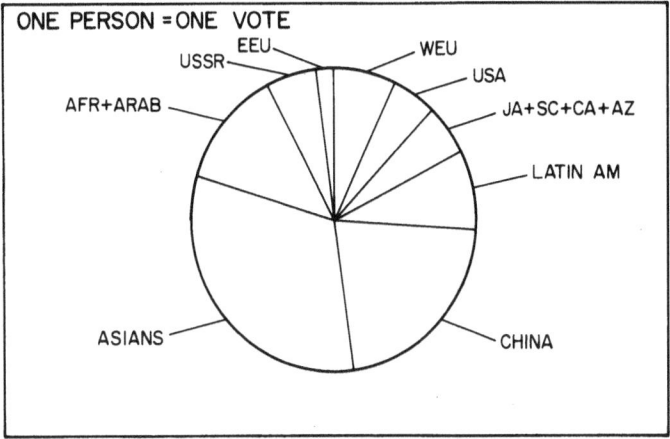

ONE PERSON = ONE VOTE

EEU
USSR
WEU
USA
AFR+ARAB
JA+SC+CA+AZ
LATIN AM
ASIANS
CHINA

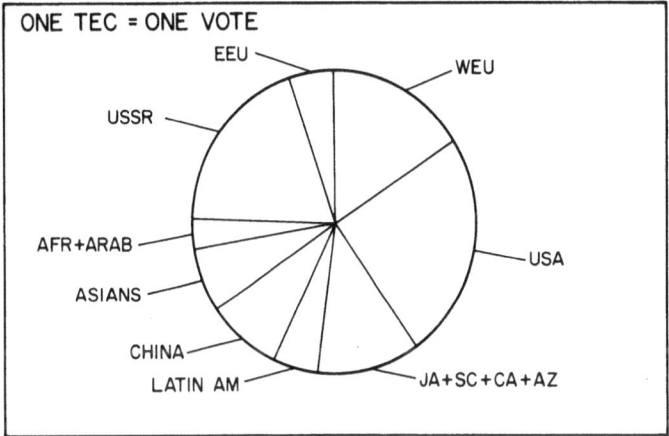

ONE TEC = ONE VOTE

EEU
WEU
USSR
AFR+ARAB
ASIANS
CHINA
USA
LATIN AM
JA+SC+CA+AZ

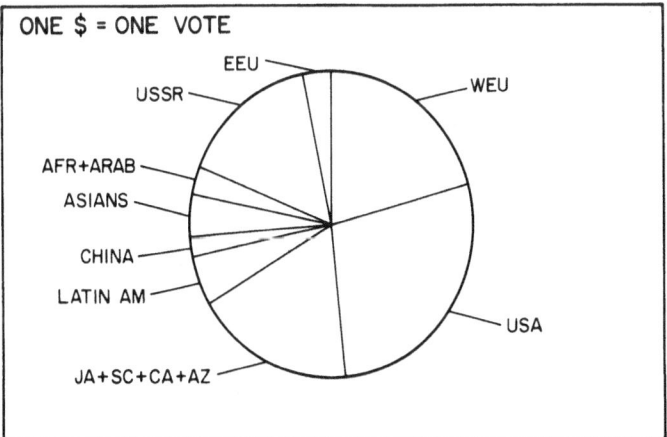

ONE $ = ONE VOTE

EEU
USSR
WEU
AFR+ARAB
ASIANS
CHINA
LATIN AM
USA
JA+SC+CA+AZ

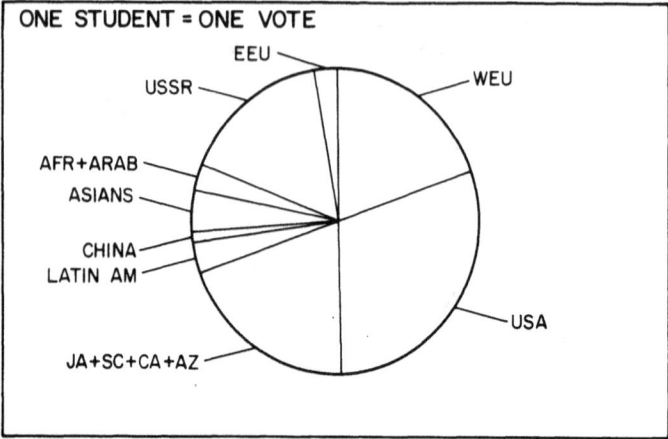

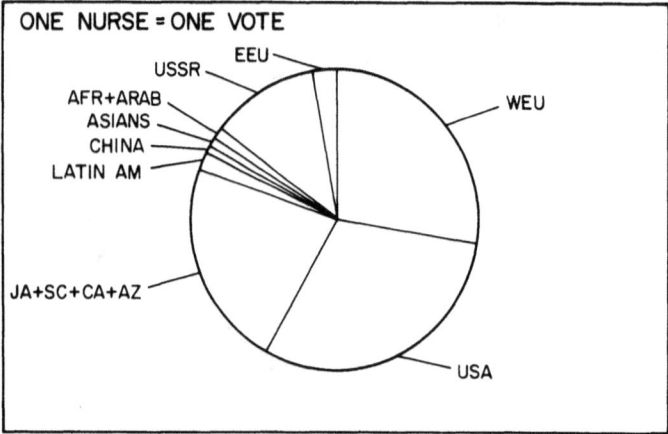

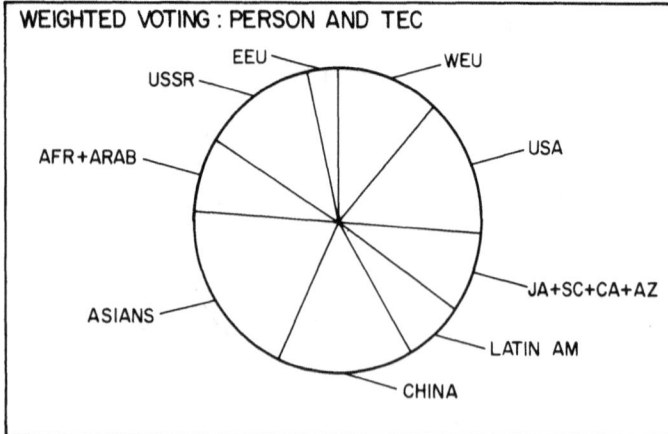

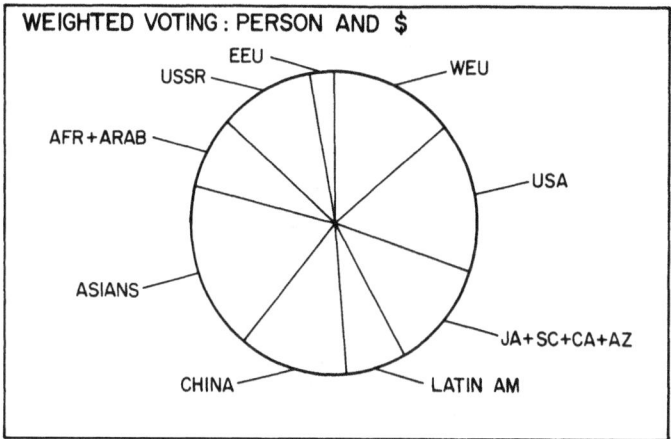

WEIGHTED VOTING : PERSON AND $

EEU
USSR
WEU
AFR+ARAB
USA
ASIANS
JA+SC+CA+AZ
CHINA
LATIN AM

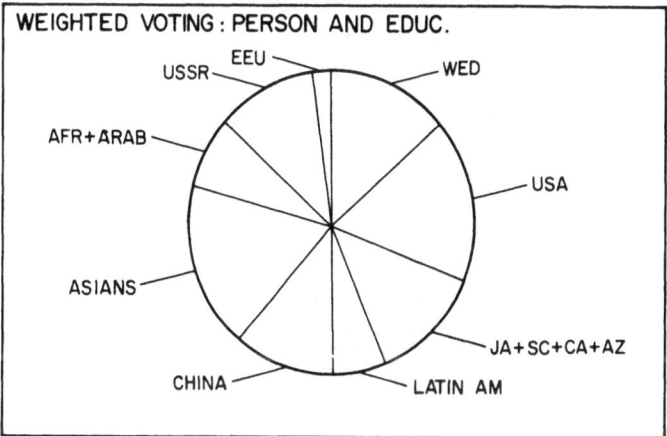

WEIGHTED VOTING : PERSON AND EDUC.

EEU
USSR
WED
AFR+ARAB
USA
ASIANS
JA+SC+CA+AZ
CHINA
LATIN AM

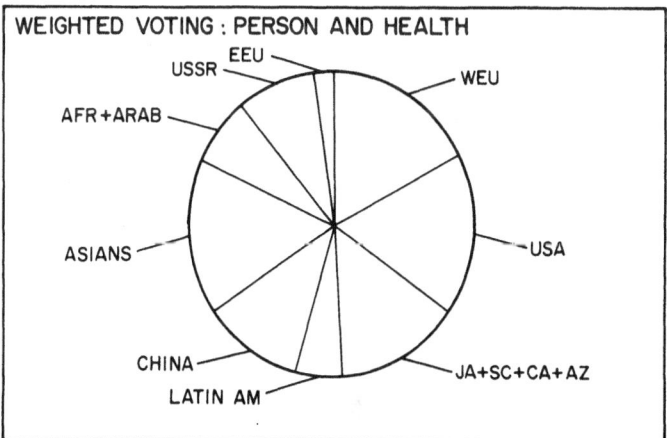

WEIGHTED VOTING : PERSON AND HEALTH

EEU
USSR
WEU
AFR+ARAB
USA
ASIANS
JA+SC+CA+AZ
CHINA
LATIN AM

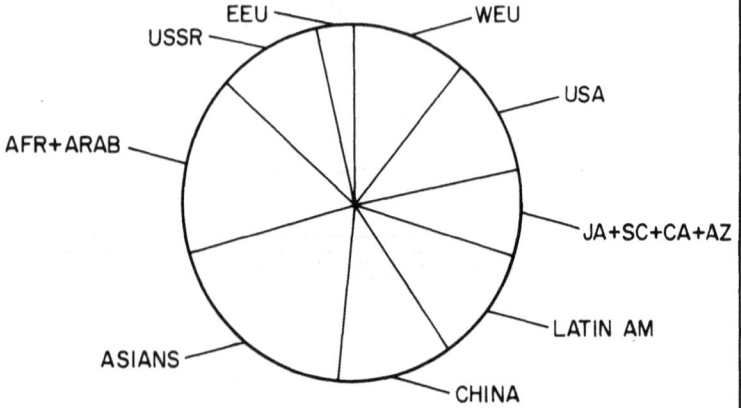

FLAG, PERSON AND TEC (USSR = 3)

EEU — USSR — AFR+ARAB — ASIANS — CHINA — LATIN AM — JA+SC+CA+AZ — USA — WEU

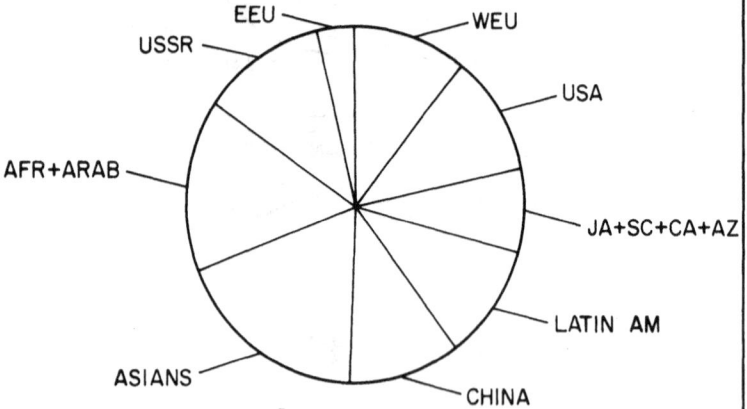

FLAG PERSON AND TEC (USSR = 15)

EEU — USSR — AFR+ARAB — ASIANS — CHINA — LATIN AM — JA+SC+CA+AZ — USA — WEU

PART IV. — VALUES AND COOPERATION

Values Needed For Survival

ERIKA ERDMANN*

"Human values, viewed in objective scientific perspective, stand out as the most strategically powerful causal control force now shaping world events." — Roger Sperry (1981)

A.   In Search of Values for Human Survival

The relinquishment of nuclear weapons is essential to prevent our species from perishing. But it is not enough. If the attitudes and values persist that led to the development of nuclear weapons in the first place, these weapons will be relinquished only to be replaced by more devious and more dangerous ones.

Chemical and bacteriological weapons can be developed with more secrecy and at less cost, and the latter, unlike nuclear weapons, can spread through infection. It would be clearly insane to use them, but no one knows what human beings are capable of doing if in despair.

Therefore, the quest for values that would prevent despair and lead mankind toward sanity has to become our first priority. You might assume, as I did, that this truth appears so obvious

---

* Part A is an adaptation of a presentation to the Canadian Peace Research and Education Association at McMaster University in Hamilton, Ontario, Canada on June 7, 1987. The research report discussed is available from University Microfilms International, 300 N. Zeeb Rd., Ann Arbor, MI 48106 (Order Number LDO1257) or from the Peace Research Institute-Dundas, 25 Dundana Ave. , Dundas, Canada L9H 4E5.

that every capable person, and especially every philosopher on earth, would be preoccupied with the search for such values.

I was, therefore, shocked to discover upon inquiries at the department of philosophy at one of the best known universities on the North American continent, that in 1981 nobody there had even thought about that question – 35 years after the first nuclear bombs had exploded and 9 years after the Club of Rome had discovered that resources on our globe are limited.

Values? Yes, they were taught, based on ancient theories, on new discoveries about the biological nature of human beings, on Church dogma, on egoism, on altruism – on everything except the need of our species to go on living.

"Does not anyone here teach ethics with the aim of human survival?" I asked – only to be met with vacant stares. Occasionally someone seemed to understand and I heard responses such as : "You ask the most important question on earth, but we are not the right place." No one could tell me where that place was.

Subsequently I searched for an entire year, receiving 84 negative responses to 84 requests that I be allowed to pursue a research project: *In Search of Values for Human Survival* within the framework of any institution. (I was warned that I would be considered a freak if I went ahead on my own.)

Finally, it was Hanna and Alan Newcombe, co-directors of the Peace Research Institute-Dundas, who offered their advice. Also, I received permission from the Columbia Pacific University to pursue my suggested research project for a Ph.D. degree.

That project consisted of a survey asking three questions:

1. What are the values needed for the survival of mankind?
2. What are the possibilities and limitations of human nature?
3. What is the best way to implement needed new values?

If we are to escape the deadlock in which we are caught, these three questions must be asked simultaneously. About values in isolation we know everything. The Golden Rule has been taught in all parts of the world for almost two thousand years – yet wars have become more devastating. To survive as a species, we must ask, "Why?"

Leading personalities in ten sectors of our society were contacted. The first five sectors were Religion, Philosophy, Science, the Humanities and the Mass Media – all those consolidating our present attitudes. The last five sectors comprised persons concerned with our future: persons promoting Science-Religion Interaction, Peace, a Sustainable Society, Technological Progress, and "Other Concerned Persons".

Each individual questioned received a typed, personal letter, accompanied by a printed questionnaire containing the three questions asked and explaining the project. In addition, because I anticipated that the expected answer rate would be only about 12 in 1000, an answer sheet was provided that could be checked by anyone too busy to answer otherwise. These answer sheets were intentionally designed to provoke thought.

All these efforts led to an overall response rate of 30.9%, much higher than expected. Altogether 221 answers were received, many of them from well-known and extremely busy persons. Not only did valuable comments arrive in abundance, but also letters, articles, and books. Of the latter, many more were recommended. The numbers of responses per sector are presented in Table I.

Table I.

Sector	Number
Peace	118
Science-Religion Interaction	113
Religion	109
Other Concerned Persons	107
Sustainable Society (Futurists I)	98
Philosophers	88
Technological Progress (Futurists II)	87
Science	80
Humanities	54
Media	22

The aim was to receive for adequate comparison at least 20 responses for each sector; Table II shows the number of letters needed to achieve this aim. Thus to receive 20 responses from the mass media, 128 letters had to be written to different persons; to receive 20 responses from the peace sector, only 32 letters were needed.

Table II.

Peace	32:20
Science Religion Interaction	37:20
Religion	41:20
Other Concerned Persons	43:20
Futurists I (Sustainable Society)	52:20
Philosophy	62:20
Futurists II (Technology)	63:20
Science	70:20
Humanities	96:20
Mass Media	128:20

Table II shows the response rate of each of the 10 sectors approached, and thus roughly indicates the rate of interest in values for human survival. The Peace sector with a 61.1% response rate was the highest, followed closely by persons promoting Science-Religion Interaction, Religion, "Other Concerned Persons," promoters of a Sustainable Society, Philosophers, promoters of Technological Progress, Scientists, and, a considerable step below, Humanists, and finally (much lower again) the Mass Media (with a response rate of 15.4%). In all sectors, females seemed clearly more alert to these problems than males.

However, statistics were of subordinate importance to the project. It is not the quantity of responses which matters, it is their quality. One answer among thousands can be the key to the door into a new world. Therefore, contemplation and comparison of individual responses was used to evaluate results.

The task was fascinating. Space does not permit a summary of even the most important answers; a few sample responses are provided at the end of the paper, but significant contributions were received from every single sector.

Religion provided the insight that: "The fate of God and the fate of those who people the earth are joined inextricably." That insight brings religion and science into a common camp. We will perish if ideals are pursued at the expense of objective truth. We will perish if objective truth is pursued at the expense of ideals.

That viewpoint is at present determining the life and work of an entire sector of our population addressed through my project, the "Promoters of science-religion interaction," from whom I received the most understanding support.

Responses from i.e. Science, Peace, etc. alone varied between extremes of optimism and pessimism. On the one hand, hope was expressed that open-mindedness and an increase of our thinking skills will lead us to as yet unknown solutions to our present problems. On the other hand it was maintained that: "There is nothing to indicate that man deserves to survive." That answer shook me profoundly. It clearly shows that not all the weapons in the world can save a humanity that loses its own sense of worth.

· In contrast to this abandonment of our species, the peace sector provided hope, most concentrated in the words of Robert Muller, the former Assistant Secretary-General of the United Nations, who said to humanity: "Do not despair, but learn."

A third sector, outstanding through its realistic global and future consciousness, was the one including promoters of a sustainable society. With one exception, all respondents from this sector knew that it is not constant population increase alone (as many scientists and humanists believe) which will degrade and destroy the lives of future generations; nor is it greed and waste of resources alone (as many religious persons and social scientists maintain). It is both. But will human nature be able to adjust itself to these two prerequisites for a safer and better world?

The anthropologist N. Graburn (University of California at Berkeley) found, based on his readings and field studies, that the key ingredient of human nature all over the globe is the *Will to Power*. "Unfortunately perhaps, persons and societies without the will to power have not survived," he says, "but those who have it may not survive either."

Another anthropologist, M. Konner (Emery University, Atlanta, GA), studying the problem from a different angle, however, sees a way out. He describes thorough research projects which prove that in widely divergent regions on earth, males have been found to be more aggressive than females. Instead of ascribing that fact to education alone, Konner admits the probability that it is an intrinsic part of being male and recommends a greater participation of females in all decision making processes. As this example shows, not rejection of inconvenient facts, but their acknowledgment and their use to build a better world will lead us forward.

Another example of this kind is G.T.L. Land's acceptance of the urge in human nature to *Grow or Die* (the title of his book). We cannot accept stagnation. We cannot abolish the urge to grow without abolishing mankind with it – but, as Land maintains, we can and must transform predominantly material growth into predominantly psychosocial growth.

Ninety-nine percent of all species evolved have perished through progress in the wrong direction. Non-human life has no choice; but with the evolution of a brain capable of love, capable of foresight, capable of visions dimly discerning its tremendous promise, human beings have been provided with the option of influencing the direction of their species' progress.

Impressive displays of the use of that option are revealed throughout my project. One of the most profound and compelling, which affirms the power of values from within the worldview of science, was recommended by a respondent from the sector "other concerned persons". It is contained in the book

Science and Moral Priority by R.W. Sperry (1983, 1985) and is quoted at the head of this paper. Let us now look at the values most likely to shape events to humanity's advantage. What do the results of my project indicate?

1. To master our fate, we must learn not to reject inconvenient facts, but to use them as building blocks for a better future.

2. Identical aims and identical values will lead to contrasting recommendations for action if perceptions of reality differ. Therefore, our concern with values has to be extended to include concern with the perception of reality from which these values arise and through which they are interpreted.

3. Except for some key values, such as wisdom, nearly all values are context-dependent and interrelated. Intelligence without love will destroy. Love without responsibility will degrade. Together, all three become components of wisdom and will elevate mankind.

The following diagram, showing the recommended values divided into those contributing to wisdom and those generated by it, has been designed by Hanna Newcombe, who came to my help when I was struggling to describe the relation of all suggested values to the best advantage for our future.

Our future depends upon the replacement of erroneous beliefs with agreement on indisputable facts. Objective search for such facts demands mental maturity. The most urgent necessity, therefore, is the provision of an adequate forum to those who would lead us toward greater mental maturity.

My project shows that these persons are there – that they exist in every sector of our society – and undoubtedly in other societies also. The humble size of the project makes that finding the more significant. Many important thoughts must have been missed.

In conclusion, I repeat, we are responsible for the fate of our earth and the fate of future generations. To achieve this we must not only abolish nuclear weapons, but also find universally acceptable values leading to a life worthy of human beings.

As the present project shows, the discovery , acceptance and effectiveness of such values is impeded through contrasting assumptions about basic aspects of reality. Top priority must therefore be given to values promoting closer approach to the truth.

Relationship Between Values

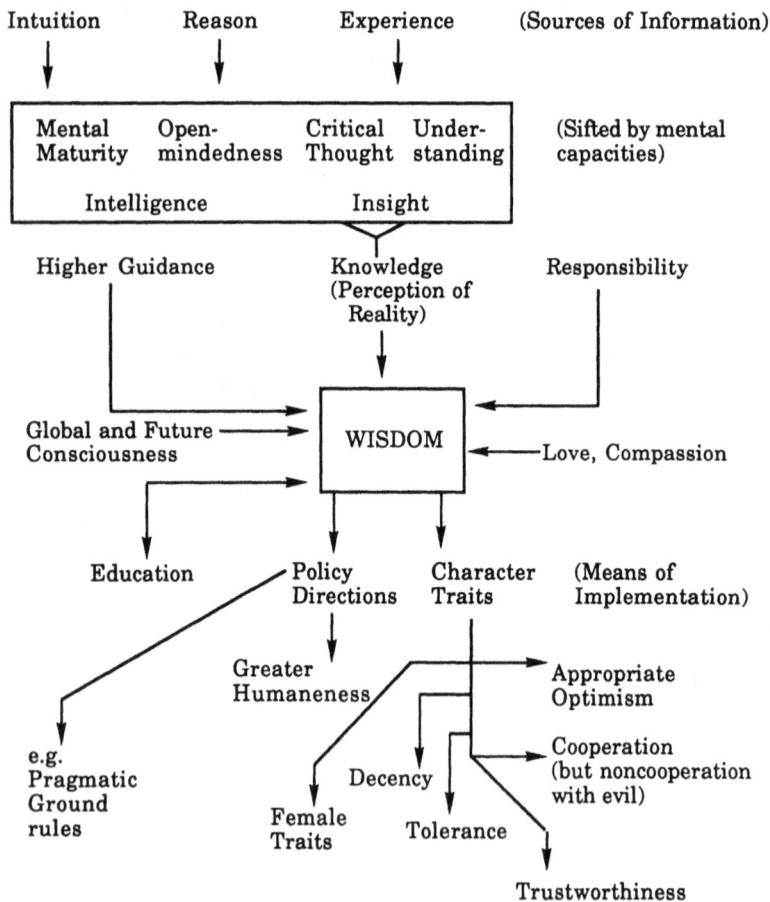

A few sample responses will conclude the project report. Some of these were elicited through the questionnaire directly, others were contained in books or papers sent or recommended by responders. Not all of them are positive – but, mirroring the diversity of human thought, they highlight our hopes and fears regarding the future.

Sample Responses

1. *Religion:* "None of us knows a sure way through our present moment in history. Those dogmatists who think they know are the greatest danger to us all. We must, therefore, work together toward the common goal and the common good, drawing upon whatever resources – religious or secular, philosophical or poetic, mythic or scientific – are available to us, and offering them to each other as we grope toward an unknown future." Kaufman, G.D., *Theology for a Nuclear Age* (1985)

2. *Philosophy:* "At the present time, mankind needs neither more nor less than some basic pragmatic ground rules promoting sustainability, development, equity, and policies which bring about positive-sum results. Anything less could fail to cope with trends which frustrate universal human values and produce conditions in which further millions if not billions live and die in conditions of desperation, stagnation and injustice. Anything more than the adoption of such ground rules would constitute attempts of social engineering and ideological imperialism. They could produce more harm than good." Laszlo, E., *The Inner Limits of Mankind* (1978)

3. *Science:* "I am optimistic because I have experienced so much progress in open-mindedness . . . If we train as many persons as we can – and all these train other persons again and so on – tens of millions of people will become much more open in their thinking and will be in a far better position to solve global problems that seem unsolvable to us now . . .

If we teach people how to think and these thinkers interact, some of them will find solutions we are unable to see now." Paul MacCready, US engineer and innovator

4. *The Humanities:* ". . . starry-eyed liberal attempts to regard every problem as a 'global' problem are very destructive." Response from an American Humanist Periodical Editor

5. *The Mass Media:* "Who will . . . decide the fate of our species? In the immediate future perhaps a dozen men at most, some of them undoubtedly mad . . . but we must look elsewhere for a tolerable life. We must count on the maturing sanity of mankind as a whole . . ." Hutchison, B. (Editor Emeritus of one of the largest Canadian newspapers), *The Unfinished Country* (1985)

6. *Science-Religion Interaction:* 1) "We need fear only our failure to keep searching for that which reality (we could translate this as nature or God) will require for continuing life." Burhoe, R.W. (Recipient of Templeton Prize for Progress in Religion), *War, Peace and Religion's Biocultural Evolution* (1986).
2) "Let me close by re-emphasizing a value that is especially dear to scientists: The habit of truth. Experience has taught scientists that in their area (in contrast to many other human activities) distortion of the facts does not pay, for nature always has the last word. The same value is also relevant for the problem to achieve a more just society." Davis, B., *Evolution, Human Diversity and Society* (1976)

7. *Peace:* "Our new global living is so sudden, so complex, so manifold and mindboggling, it is such a mixture of small and big, global and local, past and future, young and old, that our bewilderment and anxiety are not surprising but rather normal." Robert Muller (Former Assistant Secretary-General of the United Nations), *New Genesis* (1982)

8. *Sustainable Society:* 1) "There appear to be at least three tests that can be applied – not to whether a picture of reality is

'correct', but to whether it seems to be a wholesome one for society to hold. These are:

a) Does the view in the long run lead to societal or system adaptability, and hence toward survivability There are certain laws of nature and universal properties of systems that a society ignores at its peril . . .

b) Does the view lead toward fruition of the long-term trend of human civilization?

c) Is the view compatible with whatever can be discovered to be man's fundamental nature? . . ."

W.W. Harman (President of the Institute of Noetic Sciences), *A More Fundamental Look at our Energy-Environment Dilemma* (1980) 2) "One problem with the free market is that it is no respecter of carrying capacity. Only when the system collapses and prices soar does the market 'know' that anything has gone 'wrong'. Many social institutions have time horizons so short that they are irrelevant to humanity's most pressing problems. The ultimate importance of religious institutions' role in the transition rests partly on the Church's ability to compensate for that shortsightedness." Brown, R. (Director of the World Watch Institute), *Building a Sustainable Society* (1981)

9. *Technological Progress:* "When we say that honest men earn more money than dishonest men, the hearer understands us because he can think of many ways of testing this claim." "Conscience has no observable referent and is therefore meaningless." "It will be some time until the majority of political theorists realize that political science should merely aid men to do what they already want to do and that the problem of whether what they want to do is ethical is nonsensical." Beckwith, B.P., *Religion, Philosophy and Science* (1957)

10.*Other Concerned Persons:* "The tremendous power of human values to mold world conditions and decide the course of history can hardly be overstated. Human values shape human decisions that in turn govern human destiny. Any handle on human values becomes a potential handle on the future. It follows that to turn the menacing tide of spiraling population and corollary disaster trends, we need not wait for a nuclear holocaust, global famine, massive irreversible destruction of a species, life-support systems, and the like. A mere shift of human values will do it." Sperry, R.W. (Nobel Laureate in Medicine), *Science and Moral Priority* (1983, 1985)

B.   "Humankind Advancing"

One consequence of the project described was a transformation of my perception of reality: an increase of my sensitivity to factors relevant to the survival of our species and to the quality of that survival. The recognition of pertinent facts or points of view in everything I read and heard had become instant and automatic. To instil global and future consciousness, projects similar to the one described are therefore highly recommended.

Another consequence was the recurrent question whether the human species might not be genetically predisposed for self-destruction. That question frightened me the more, the more often I rediscovered it expressed by persons of outstanding capabilities and in leading positions.

"Intelligence", a professor of chemical physics at the California Institute of Technology said, "is the most dangerous product of evolution." It is the result of the fiercest competition, he believes, and the population of our earth is unable to generate enough wisdom to defuse its destructive thrust. (Kupperman, 1987)

Another leading senior scientist, associated with NASA, reports about belief among persons of his stature in the possibility that a "cosmic principle of self-destruction" could prevent advances of civilization, not only here on earth but on other planets too, through a drive toward complexity that runs out of control. It is estimated that such a principle will operate regularly a few decades after a given civilization begins to encounter worldwide problems, a time period that started here on earth, according to the estimate of the author, about ten years ago. (Chaisson, 1988)

Such thoughts are haunting enough. They are superseded, however, by the belief that our species not only *cannot* survive, but that it *must* not survive. Consider the conviction that "we are pollution" by someone who is "appalled by all that an insane humanity may yet survive to do," and the letter of a medical student to his father, stating that, "We're destroying the planet, there's not a damn thing that can be done about it. It's going to be very slow, drawn out and ugly or so fast it doesn't make any difference," (Falk, 1979). These statements may – as yet – be the voices of isolated fanatics. But these voices are generated by facts, and they may have consequences too frightening to think about.

In my view, such loss of faith in humanity is a danger, greater than either the threat of nuclear warfare or the threat of environmental degradation: loss of faith in humanity paralyzes the very will to counter these threats.

How can justified regard for humankind be strengthened? How can confidence in its potentials be resurrected? How can we advance toward more farsighted, responsible attitudes?

Heroic efforts to join facts and values fall apart as preferences for either one or the other side predominate. Spokesmen or women for mature points of view, desperately needed pilots of humanity, remain unheard; their voices drown in the turmoil of short-range concerns and interminable power struggles in every field and at every level.

Professor W. Basil McDermott, a deep and thorough thinker who is lecturing on our future at Simon Fraser University in Burnaby, B.C., Canada, believes that the very absence of positive results proves that we are on the wrong track altogether. Unless we can discover new thoughts we don't yet know how to think, we will merely perpetuate and increase misery on earth. He says:

"If one accepts the dominant projections if not aspirations for the future of our world as producing an increasingly complex and interdependent system of life on the planet the tensions, conflicts, problems, and tragedies involved in this overarching vision of necessary control may be so far-reaching that the relatively mild and periodic ambivalence we today may express towards the termination of life on earth, however achieved, might become a commonplace longing in a future world with much greater misery than our own. As we lose our patience with contemporary methods to reduce human   misery, we become more vulnerable to a longing for the sufferings of this world to be extinguished once and for all."

Will we discover the new thoughts we need before despair becomes dominant? I do not know . But I cannot cease to work toward that hope. My thinking is guided by the conclusion from my project that the most urgent necessity is the provision of an adequate forum to those who would lead us toward greater mental maturity.

If the voices of rivals, each of whom has something important to contribute to our endangered world, could be combined into a strong substrate of human wisdom; if, instead of squandering their rare capabilities on priority fights, they could be made or be shown to mutually support one another . . .

I founded a Quarterly, called *Humankind Advancing*, targeted mainly toward university libraries, and containing, in the form of quotes, excerpts, reviews or short original contributions, whatever can be found that would lead our species toward greater mental maturity.

Its title page portrays a ship, desperate for pilots, being driven toward unknown and unseen dangers.

Notes

Beckwith, B.B.: *Religion, Philosophy, and Science.* New York: Philosophical Library (1957).

Brown, L.R.: *Building a Sustainable Society.* New York: Norton (1981).

Burhoe, R.W.: *War, Peace and Religion's Biocultural Evolution.* Zygon, 21: 439-472 (1986).

Chaisson, E.J. : *Our Cosmic Heritage*, Zygon, 23: 469-479 (1988).

Davis, B. : *Evolution, Human Diversity, and Society*, Zygon, 11: 80-95 (1976).

Erdmann, E.: *In Search of Values for Human Survival*, Ann Arbor: University Microfilms International (1987).

Erdmann, E.: *Challenge to Humanity: Values for Survival and Progress*, Peace Research Institute-Dundas, Canada (1989).

Falk. R.A.: *Foreword*, The Global Predicament. D.W. Orr and M.S. Soroos, (Eds.), p. xii, Chapel Hill: University of North Carolina Press (1979).

Graburn, N.: *Contribution to Challenge to Humanity: Values for Survival and Progress*, by E. Erdmann (p. 63). Peace Research Institute-Dundas, Canada (1989).

Harman, W.W.: *A More Fundamental Look at our Energy-Environment Dilemma*, W.W. Harman, Institute of Noetic Science, 475 Gate Five Road, Suite 300, Sausalito, CA 94965 USA (1980).

Humankind Advancing. E. Erdmann (Ed.), R.R. 1, Lockeport, N.S. B0T 1LO, Canada.

Hutchison, B.: *The Unfinished Country*, Vancouver, B.C.: Douglas McIntyre (1985).

Kaufman, G.D.: *Technology for a Nuclear Age*, Philadelphia, PA: Westminster Press (1985).

Konner, M.: *The Tangled Wing*, New York: Harper & Row (1982).

Kupperman, A.: *Cosmology, the Origin of Life, Evolution and Religion*, Lecture at the California Institute of Technology on February 12, 1987.

Laszlo, E.: *The Inner Limits of Mankind*, Elmsford, N.J.: Pergamon Press (1978).

MacCready, P. : *Contribution to Challenge to Humanity: Values for Survival and Progress*, by E. Erdmann (p. 48-49). Peace Research Institute-Dundas, Canada (1989).

McDermott, W. Basil: *The Future as Metaphor*, Futures (Great Britain) March 1990.

Muller, R.: *New Genesis*, Garden City, N.Y.: Doubleday (1982).

Sperry, R.W.: *Changing Priorities*, Annual Review of Neuroscience, 4: 1-15 (1981).

Sperry, R.W.: *Science and Moral Priority*, New York: Columbia University Press, Reprinted 1985 by Praeger, New York (now Greenwood, Westport, CT.) (1983).

The Roots of Cooperation

HANNA NEWCOMBE*

There are six roots of cooperation in human societies: kinship, reciprocity, contract, utility, equity, and universality. These roots range from minimal to maximal in motivation, but it is interesting that even at the reciprocity level, cooperation can be firmly and robustly established in a group.

Theoretically, the kinship principle is rooted in sociobiology, the wish to help the survival of one's genes ("extended fitness"). I share approximately half the genes with my parents and my children, a high proportion with my siblings, less with my cousins, uncles and aunts, nieces and nephews, much less with other members of my tribe, hardly any with foreigners. I will therefore practise most altruism and cooperation with the closest members of my family, somewhat less with members of the extended family, only limited cooperation with the rest of the tribe, and none (or even hostility) to strangers. This principle produces cooperation only in a limited group, not universal; concentric circles, like a Mandala, bright at the centre and quickly shading through greyness into the outer darkness. On this is based family solidarity, and in the larger realm tribalism, patriotism and nationalism: "I against my brothers; I and my brothers against our cousins; my brothers and my cousins against outsiders."

There are some difficulties in this. The family application may be clear; the biological lines of similarity are obvious and easily traced. But a tribe may have received some immigrants (it

---

* Republished from Peace Research Reviews, Vol. XI, No. 5, 1990.

certainly has by exogenous marriage), and no nation on Earth is racially pure. The application to nationalism is then definitely suspect, and based more on artificially created fiction than on natural reality. The "purpose" (excuse the teleological abbreviation) of sexual reproduction is, after all, to churn up the gene pool, not to leave the lines of descent clear and distinct. And the human gene pool has certainly been churned up, through immigration, refugees, travel and commerce (increasingly in modern times), and also through war (distant armies). As someone quipped: "soldiers drop their genes".

Secondly, the proportion of genes shared with relatives (one half, one quarter, or whatever) are not right. This applies only to the highly variable regions which define the "self" in immunology. But after all, all humans share by far most of their genome universally, because those parts define the species rather than the self. The truth is that I share 99.9% of the DNA base pair sequences even with a stranger, and maybe 99.99% with my sister; the whole proposition then becomes far less meaningful. If I truly want to preserve my genes, I must practise altruism to the whole human race. And I also share maybe 80% of my genes with other mammals, and so on down the line of all creation. This other brand of sociobiology would lead straight into universality – but I am getting ahead of myself.

The second root of cooperation is reciprocity, which is social rather than biological. The idea is that, when I do someone a favour, I expect the favour to be returned at some future time, and this is why I do it. If someone does me a favour, I feel obligated to return it at the next opportunity. The other face of reciprocity is that when someone is nasty to me, I will be nasty right back, and vice versa, I expect such punishment from others which may deter me from being nasty. Reciprocity has therefore been called "tit for tat", and Robert Axelrod has written a wonderful book about it, *The Evolution of Cooperation*.

Axelrod's book deals with a "game" situation called Prisoner's Dilemma (PD), which simulates the very common social situations in which "defection" (non-cooperation) pays off in the short run (like telling a lie or cheating), but if both participants defect, they receive less benefit than if both cooperate (tell the truth and practice honesty). But the biggest loser is the player who cooperates while the other defects. Thus there is a temptation to defect in the short run, but if players expect to meet repeatedly over the long run, it pays to cooperate.

Axelrod arranged the encounters between different strategies of playing PD (supplied by experts in the field) in a computer round-robin tournament, in which every strategy would meet every other strategy many times. It turned out, in repeated experiments, that the simplest strategy submitted, tit for tat, won (got the most points) every time. This strategy never defects first (is "nice"), always retaliates immediately after the other player's defection (is "provocable"), but retaliates only once and then returns to cooperation if the other player does (is "forgiving"). (It is taking "an eye for an eye" to signal that it will not be exploited, but never takes two eyes for one eye, i.e. does not escalate.) It is also easy to figure out by the other player (is "clear"), so that mutual learning can take place.

Axelrod also performed repeated rounds of the same tournament, in which low-scoring strategies (receiving less than a predetermined number of points) were eliminated at the end of each round, while the high-scoring strategies (receiving more than a certain upper limit of points) were allowed to "reproduce", i.e. be represented by multiple copies in the next round of the tournament. This experiment simulated the evoluton of the various strategies, with the unfit going extinct and the fittest showing reproductive success. Some strategies went to the wall almost immediately, mainly the ones that were not "nice" (i.e. defected first), because they lost too many points in being punished by the retaliators. So greed does not pay. Some other strategies increased for a while but then decreased, because the strategies against which they did well had been eliminated. Again, tit for tat was the most robust survivor. Anatol Rapoport, who submitted this strategy to the contest, explains that tit for tat does not really "win" over any other strategy; in fact, it cannot, because it only follows the other's lead. But the other strategies that can win, kill each other off, and meek little tit for tat inherits the earth. Or as Axelrod puts it, tit for tat does not win any single rounds in the sense of getting more points than the other player, but excels in eliciting cooperation from the other player, enabling both to win points. After all, PD is a non-zero-sum game, not pure conflict. You don't have to win *over* the others as in chess. But life is more like PD than like chess, most of the time.

Axelrod derives certain interesting propositions:

1. If the discount parameter w (which measures the frequency or the probability of the two players meeting again in the future) is large enough, there is no best strategy independent of the strategy used by the other player. (In other words, it depends on the social environment in which you find yourself.);

2. Tit for tat is collectively stable (i.e. it cannot be invaded by any other strategy once it is firmly established so that most players use it), *only if* w (the probability of players meeting again) is large enough. In the short term, when you don't expect to meet again very much, it is best to play all-D (defect on every move), i.e. "war of all against all";

3. The above may apply to other strategies that are "nice", i.e. cooperate on the first move and are never the first to defect. Again, the expectation of meeting again has to be large enough;

4. For a "nice" strategy to be collectively stable, it must be provoked to retaliation by the very first defection by the other player;

5. The "all-D" strategy is always collectively stable, for any value of w (i.e. whether we meet again or not). This means that a single copy of any other strategy, including tit for tat, could not successfully spread in such an environment, and would be eliminated. An isolated cooperator cannot get a

foothold in a society of "meanies". Nor can several isolated cooperators;

6. However, some strategies can invade all-D if they are in a cluster, i.e. if they interact more frequently with each other than with the more numerous "meanies", so that they can give each other some winning points. The strategies which can do this cluster invasion of all-D most easily and quickly are ones that are maximally discriminating, i.e. cooperate with their own kind and retaliate against the "meanies". Tit for tat is a maximally discriminating strategy, and can therefore successfully invade all-D in clusters;

7. If a "nice" strategy, such as tit for tat, cannot be invaded by a single individual copy of another strategy, then it cannot be invaded by a cluster of such strategies either. In particular, that means that a world of tit for tat players (acting as cooperators) cannot be invaded by all-D, either single or in clusters. Tit for tat is "robust", in addition to all its other properties (nice, provocable, forgiving, clear).

I have given a rather lengthy summary of this because Axelrod's work is not too well known yet, but it deserves to be. Summarizing the summary: In a persistent long-range interaction situation (as in a society), "nice" but "provocable" (though "forgiving") cooperation is collectively stable. A Hobbesian situation of "war of all against all" is also collectively stable, in both short- and long-lasting interactions; while it cannot be invaded by single cooperators, it can be successfully invaded by clusters of cooperators, which in time will transform the Hobbesian situation into a cooperating society. Once established, such a cooperating society cannot be successfully invaded by either single "meanies" or clusters of "meanies".

It should be remembered that this result was obtained with Prisoner's Dilemma, a game whose "rational" outcome for egoists (individual utility maximizers) is mutual defection (all-D). If anything, the experiment was biased against cooperation, and yet cooperation emerged, was able to establish itself and grow, and then resist being displaced. This is because mutual cooperation is in the long run more advantageous, even to egoists. The overall conclusion then is that cooperation can grow and be robust even in a world of egoists without central authority. Thus Hobbes' solution of the Leviathan is not necessary to cure the Hobbesian dilemma of the war of all against all. There is a "natural" (as opposed to coerced) tendency to cooperation in human societies (at least in computer situations) as the Anarchists have always maintained.

Thus reciprocity is a powerful mechanism for cooperation, more subtle and convincing than the biologically-based kinship model. However, there is an interesting example which illustrates the simultaneous operation of both kinship and reciprocity. This is the mutual feeding of female vampire bats, as described by Gerald Wilkinson in Scientific American, February 1990. These bats have to obtain a blood meal from horses or cows each night – if a bat fails to obtain a meal even two nights in succession, she starves to death. A bat who has missed a meal begs another bat to share hers, by regurgitaton. The benefactor may comply or not – it is an act of altruism on her part, because she increases her risk of starvation if she fails to obtain a meal the next night. But she is more likely to do it if either the begging bat is a relative (especially her own child, where this is done routinely), or if the two bats live in the same tree colony and therefore interact continuously over time, so that reciprocation may be expected in the future. Reciprocation in meal sharing then increases the survivability of both cooperating bats.

The third root of cooperation is social contract, usually applied and administered by what Axelrod calls "central authority", i.e. government. Although cooperation can develop spontaneously by reciprocity, as just shown, it is useful to confirm and legitimize it by an explicit contract. Contractarian theories (e.g. Hobbes, Locke, Rousseau, Rawls) deal in terms of a sociological fiction: that there was a time when humans lived together without a social contract; that they realized that all would benefit if there was a contract; and that they came together to negotiate the terms and created and ratified a contract. I think the authors all realize that this is not a historical account of events, but a convenient "creation myth". In reality, an implicit contract may have been dimly in the consciousness of a few leaders, who then started gradually enforcing it by their own absolute power based on force, either sheer military force or the authority of religion. Enlightened tyrants of this type would enforce a contract that would benefit their whole society, not just themselves. They would realize that in the long-range game of politics (if it is a Prisoner's Dilemma) it pays to cooperate with one's subjects as long as they cooperate, rather than exploit them mercilessly, because they might revolt. But never mind what *really* happened; we are interested in the contractarian fiction, because it clarifies conceptually what a social contract involves.

In this fiction, humans "in the wild" or "in a state of nature" are either intent on continual mutual robbery, murder and mayhem (as Hobbes would have it), or are "noble savages" who trust and cooperate (according to Rousseau). In either case, they are assumed to be rational, i.e. capable of making decisions to improve their condition. They decide, one and all, that they wish to form a society, and are seeking some rational rules by which that society will operate. They act "behind a veil of ignorance", in the sense that they don't know what position in the society each would get to occupy – powerful or lowly, rich or poor. They therefore strive to make it "fair" for everybody, because it is in their interest to do so, in case they end up on the bottom rung of the pecking order. They strive for "justice" in the sense of "fairness", according to John Rawls, yet not necessarily equality, because they want to balance equality with freedom, and also inequality might provide more incentives to work hard and raise the standard of living. (I find it amusing to visualize these noble or ignoble savages as already so knowledgeable about capitalist theory – budding Reaganites and Thatcherites before their time.)

In any case, the original society as created by the contract does not yet have a government. That is the next step. After that primordial contract fixes the underlying ideology (egalitarian or not, libertarian or not), the founders must then write a constitution to describe the detailed structures of government. The constitution is fundamental with respect to the particular legislation that will follow, but the social contract itself is even more fundamental than the constitution. According to John Locke, "Civil Society" pre-dates government. This has recently become the inspiration of the non-violent revolutionaries of Central and Eastern Europe in the fall of 1989. After having been crushed by a very top-heavy government for 40-45 years, they now want more power to go to spontaneous citizen organizations like Civic Forum in Czechoslovakia. The Helsinki Citizens Assembly wants this to prevail throughout the 35 nations of the Conference on Security and Cooperation in Europe (Helsinki Agreement). I can only wish them well.

There are different versions of the social contract in contractarian theories. Hobbes considers even a tyrannical "Leviathan" to be preferable to "the war of all against all", which it well might be – except that I doubt that that particular "state of nature" ever existed in history or nature. As somebody remarked, if humans had been so intent on killing each other off, they would have done it long ago and we would not be writing about it.

Rousseau considered his initial society as being "close-coupled", as I would now call it. That is, the individual wills of citizens are assumed to have merged into "the general will". In voting, each citizen will be trying to second-guess what that General Will is and vote accordingly, rather than defending his own selfish interests. Rousseau's society is thus diametrically opposed to an alternative model in which special interests (e.g. farmers, workers, industrialists, professionals, etc.) organize, and the collective decisions that emerge reflect their relative strength or power or clout through some process of hard bargaining and mutual trade-offs. Rousseau's model seems more idealistic, but as so often happens with utopian ideologies, it goes sour in practice.

The General Will is too centralizing, too oppressive. It becomes the object of idolatry. In the French Revolution it was most prominently embraced by the Jacobins, and it led to the Terror. Any dissenter from the revolutionary state was obviously not attuned to the General Will, and was therefore put to death as an enemy of society. This is a familiar pattern to us in the 20th century for various brands of totalitarianism, both left and right. Rousseau thought that he was writing a blueprint for a perfect democracy and total social harmony, but the human tendency to fanaticism when fired up with an idea led straight to absolute tyranny.

There was an alternative, even then, at the end of the 18th century. The Girondins represented federalism and the diffusion of power. The French Revolution could have taken a different turn. Closer to our own time, Stalin did not have to follow Lenin in the Russian Revolution. It could have been Trotsky. Yet I have some doubts that the Terror in both cases was the result of the depravity or fanaticism of one man, Robespierre or Stalin. It is more likely that the fault lies in the ideology itself and the fanaticism it arouses. Trotsky would not have been any less oppressive, I would think.

So one has to be very careful about the social contract. It might turn out to be Leviathan after all. But there are more benign versions. I shall look at only one more, as presented in John Rawls' book *A Theory of Justice*. There are two parts to the social contract in this version. In the first part, people agree to maximize individual freedom, i.e. to permit every member of society to do as he or she pleases as long as it does not infringe on the freedom of others. (This is the same principle as that expounded by J.S. Mill in *On Liberty*). In the second part, only as much inequality is permitted as would leave even the most disadvantaged member of society no worse off than he/she would be under conditions of equality. The assumption here is that some inequality is needed to spur production to increase the total wealth of society. So with a sufficient amount of inequality to provide incentives, the overall size of the pie will be greater. The poorest will receive a smaller slice of the pie because of the inequality, but the principle stipulates that this slice that goes to the poorest must be greater than their larger proportion of the smaller pie would be under equality. This is why, under the veil of ignorance, every member of the original contract would choose this limited degree of inequality over complete equality.

This model is thus constructed along the lines of liberal capitalism and is obviously under the influence of that ideology. Justice is seen as a compound of freedom and equality, as is quite common in political ideologies. But freedom and equality can form compounds in different proportions, like carbon and oxygen forming either CO or CO_2, and this gives us the basis of different ideologies, like capitalism or socialism. Rawls opts for one possibility which has a certain appeal. It is not unbridled capitalism because the degree of inequality permitted is limited, and there is concern for the welfare of the poor. But the thesis of Adam Smith that only selfish incentives will be a spur to production is accepted without question and the benefit of more production (i.e. growth) is also implicit. But it is now questionable whether growth beyond a certain point produces more happiness, or whether it rather depletes resources and pollutes the environment. All these considerations are not included by Rawls, and therefore his conception of justice remains just one of a series of alternatives, not necessarily the only one or the best one.

The fourth root of cooperation, utility, gave its name to Utilitarianism, the theory of the greatest happiness of the greatest number, elaborated by Jeremy Bentham and John Stuart Mill. But first I must give an introduction to the last three roots, because in going from Root 3 to Root 4, we are crossing the boundary from theories based on selfishness to theories placed on an ethical basis. From now on we do not necessarily ask: *What's in it for me?*, although we do not abandon self-interest altogether. There was already a beginning of this in contractarianism, in the concept of the General Will, but now it will become more pervasive.

Why should any of us consider the interests of others, for their own sake, not just for reasons which benefit ourselves (such as kinship, reciprocity, or contract)? The answer is not easy to express in words, though I feel it strongly, almost like an axiom in geometry. Of course it is not an axiom because some people do not find it to be self-evident. It is this: other people, all people, have the same essence that I have, consist mentally and spiritually of the same "stuff" as I, and therefore deserve the same care and consideration that I lavish on myself. Just to have a name for it, I will call it "the Principle of the Shared Essence" (PSE). Quakers might say: *There is that of God in every person*, but I don't want to make this dependent on religion.

Returning to utilitarianism, in saying that the aim of our actions should be the securing of the greatest happiness of the greatest number of people, we have widened the meaning of "utility" from the selfish utility maximization of the "rational player" of Prisoner's Dilemma (or of Adam Smith's "economic man") to the maximization of collective utility. If people played PD in this frame of mind, they would cooperate automatically without any dilemma, and Axelrod's elaborate mechanisms would be unnecessary, as would any contract or central authority. This would be part of Level 6 of Kohlberg's scale of moral judgement, namely principled conscience. (The lower levels, starting with 1, are fear of punishment, seeking approval, conformity, respect for law and order and social contract. Some of these may correlate with the "roots" in our previous discussion, e.g. conformity with reciprocity, social contract with social contract.)

Some precautions are needed in fostering other people's happiness. The main one is that we should not give them what we think is good for them, but what they themselves tell us they want for their own happiness. It would be no use giving classical records to someone who likes rock and roll, or serve a nice juicy steak to a vegetarian. My friend Don Bryant, who has done a lot of thinking and writing about the philosophy of altruism, recommends leaving a portion of our "sphere of interests" empty (as a "crypt of disinterest") for other people to fill – only this would be true altruism.

However, there is a more fundamental problem. In striving for the greatest happiness of the greatest number, we are trying to maximize the sum of everybody's utilities. I will leave aside the vexing problem of whether individual utilities can be intersubjectively compared or added together; this problem is rather abstract. I am more concerned with a practical problem: I may be able to maximize the sum by taking away some happiness from one person in order to give a greater amount of happiness to another person. But is this "fair"? Or in the extreme case, I may be able to increase the security of the state by sending a few recalcitrants to the guillotine, and here we go again down the slippery slope to terror and tyranny. For the sake of greatest happiness, mind you! Something is terribly wrong.

The trouble is that maximizing the sum of everyone's utilities is not enough, we must also have some rules about the distribution of happiness among the people. We might add some absolute prohibitions, in the form of a few core human rights: freedom from extra-judicial or arbitrary killing, freedom from torture and cruel treatment, freedom from arbitrary arrest and detention, freedom from hunger, freedom from discrimination; or my even shorter list: no genocide, no torture, no disappearance, no death squads, no starvation, no apartheid. The trouble with lists is that you are apt to forget some important item. And it is no use lengthening the list too much either; the Universal Declaration of Human Rights has 30 articles, but not all can be fulfilled in practice, especially by the very poor countries.

Alternatively, we might proclaim that human life is sacred and must never be touched – an absolute tabu. But we would run into problems in medical ethics. Which patient will get the organ transplant when these are scarce, which patient will get scarce resources like a kidney machine, and will a patient be allowed to die without heroic measures if he/she wants to? In practice, there must be some trade-offs sometimes.

Another approach might be to say that we should never take an action that makes even one person even a little bit less happy than before. We are allowed only to take actions that increase someone's happiness while leaving others at least the same as before. But this may be too stringent. If we are on a sight-seeing tour and my two-year-old starts to cry that he wants to go home, I should not spoil everyone else's enjoyment by insisting that the tour bus go back at once. I bundle up the child and take him along anyway, knowing that he will soon forget the incident and be happy again.

We need some measure of fairness or equity to supplement our utility principle. And this takes us to the fifth root of cooperation which we call equity. Note that we are not replacing the maximum utility principle, but adding to it. The sense of equity as fairness is actually very commonly observed. People play some non-zero-sum games not as selfish maximizers exclusively, but they do sometimes what would be fair to the other player, especially if it does not cost them much. And children at play are constantly shrieking "that's not fair", assuming that the other child knows what that means.

Under the utility principle, the rule was to maximize the sum of all utilities. What we now need to do under the equity principle is to minimize the differences between individual utilities. We do not say that everyone's utilities should be equal – which probably cannot be done – but that we should strive to minimize the differences. For example, someone with a disability, let us say in a wheelchair, will be less happy than a walking person, other things being equal. We try to even things out for the disabled person by providing wheelchair access to all buildings, even though this costs taxpayers some money.

Maximizing the sum of two numbers while simultaneously minimizing their difference means that we maximize the product. Try it: 1+9, 2+8, 3+7, 4+6, 5+5 all add up to 10; but the products are 9, 18, 21, 24, 25. The largest product is obtained when the difference is smallest. For the same reason, of all quadrilaterals with the same perimeter, the square has the largest area. Though we will not prove it here, the same rule applies when we are adding or multiplying more than two numbers. Maximizing the product is associated with the "Nash solution" in economics and decision theory, and this is what we are adopting here.

The sixth and final root of cooperation is universality, which simply means including everybody in the calculations of utility and equity, not only those "playing the game at the time", i.e. narrowly and locally concerned. Universality is already implied in the PCE (Principle of Common Essence) – *all* humans are made of the same stuff, and deserve the same response, as the present players in a situation. But PCE is also strongly implied in equity (the innate sense of fairness) and in collective utility. PCE encompasses all three of the higher roots of cooperation.

We have discussed universality as extending to all humans, but it should also be extended to all living creatures, with appropriate discounting factors, because their "essence", while similar to ours, is not quite identical. The discounting factors would differ from one species to another. They might depend on the degree of their consciousness or intelligence (except that we only guess at this and don't know it), or the degree of relatedness to us (sociobiology again). We have to leave these concepts a bit vague, but insist that all living creatures should be included in some way in our utility calculations, in order to satisfy the requirement of universality.

With universality capping collective utility and equity, we have a PCE-based complex which can be called Agape (universal love). It is "rational agape" in the sense that we do not emotionally love all those people out there – we cannot, because we have not even met them. But we do recognize their claim to life and to quality of life as being just as valid as our own. We do this rationally and out of a sense of fairness. This has been expressed in various moral rules, such as: "Do unto others what you want them to do unto you". This is the Christian wording of the *Golden Rule*, but the same thought has been formulated by all the higher religions. Immanuel Kant's "categorical imperative" ("so act that you would be willing to have everyone act that way") is a way of explicitly universalizing the moral value of your actions. Kant also said: "Never use any human being as a means; always treat him/her as an end". Martin Buber would add: "Every human being is a Thou, not an It", which is an admirable way of stating the *Principle of Common Essence*. J.S. Woodsworth, the founder of the CCF party in Canada (now the NDP) said: "What we want for ourselves , we want for all". This is the same principle as Gandhi's Sarvodaya, which means "the welfare of all". Needless to say, any of these rules would abolish the dilemma in PD without any "strategies" being necessary. As guides to action, they all simply say "cooperate".

However, rational agape can be further intensified if we add empathy, meaning that we rejoice when others are happy and mourn when others suffer. This is a feeling, not reason. Most people are genuinely saddened or outraged or moved to action (helping behaviour) when they see television pictures of starving Ethiopians. People's spirits are lifted in watching a joyous celebration with music and happy faces. We can summarize this by saying that rational agape plus empathy equals integral agape, the highest motivation for cooperation that we can have. It involves not only reason, but feeling and will as well – in fact, our whole being. It would be Kohlberg's stage 7, which Kohlberg did not even describe. As Paul said: "The greatest of these is Love".

Notes

1. Axelrod, Robert. *The Evolution of Cooperation*, Basic Books, New York 1984, 241 pp.

2. Bryant, Don, *Altruism: Judging Motivation*, Paper for Canadian Peace Research and Education Conference, Univ. of Saskatchewan, Saskatoon, 1979.

3. Buber, Martin, *I and Thou*, Scribner, New York, 1970.

4. Hobbes, Thomas, *Leviathan*, J.M. Dent, 1914, London.

5. Kant, Immanuel, *Critique of Practical Reason*, Garland, New York, 1976.

6. Kohlberg, Lawrence, *Collected Papers on Moral Development and Moral Education*, Harvard University Press, Cambridge, MA., 1973.

7. Mill, John Stuart, *Utilitarianism*, Bobb's-Merrill, Indianapolis, 1971.

8. Mill, John Stuart, *On Liberty*, H. Davidson. Arlington Heights, IL, 1989.

9. Rawls, John, *A Theory of Justice*, Belknap Press, Harvard University Press, Cambridge, MA 1971, 607 pp.

10. Rousseau, Jean-Jacques, *Social Contract and Discourses*, Fitzhenry and Whiteside, Markham, Ont., 1979, 380 pp.

11. Wilkinson, Gerald, *Food Sharing in Vampire Bats*, Scientific American, February, 1990. pp. 76-82.

PART V. — ECOLOGICAL ISSUES

Climatic Crisis: A World Federalist Response

CHARLOTTE WATERLOW

A. The Context

Since the climatic threat is the most menacing feature of a looming world crisis which affects all aspects of human life, let us first briefly put it in context.

The world's population, which it is estimated was around 1.7 billion in 1900, reached 2.5 billion in 1950 and 5.3 billion in 1990. According to the United Nations projections, it could reach 6.5 billion by the year 2000, and stabilize at around 10 billion by about the middle of the 21st century.

Seventy-five per cent of the world's population live in the developing countries, where in general "basic needs" are not met, and in particular 1.5 billion people live in abject poverty. By the year 2050, 90% of the world's population, 8.5 billion people, will be living in the developing countries.

The industrialized countries, with 25% of the world's population, today consume 80% of the world's resources, possess 80% of its income, eat 50% of its food, produce 90% of its manufactures and do 95% of its research. Two billion people in the developing countries have no access to electricity and use wood for heating and cooking.

While needs are exploding, resources are diminishing. Food supplies are threatened by desertification, deforestation and pollution. Non-renewable resources, such as oil and certain key minerals, are running out, and coal is now climatically disastrous. Arms production is diverting essential resources and brain power to unproductive ends.

The process of unbridled economic "growth", launched by the Industrial Revolution, has become cancerous. It is essential to planetary health to move into a new era in which world resources are equitably shared in accordance with humanity's basic needs. The Brundtland Report of 1987 on *Environment and Development* calls for "sustainable development", defined as "progress in all countries that meets the needs of the present without compromising the ability of future generations to meet their own needs". The current concepts of "growth" and "development" will have to be reformulated.

B.   The Nature of the Climatic Threat

The world's climate has been stable since the last Ice Age ended 5 to 10,000 years ago. Now as a result of human activities, it is suddenly threatened with two fundamental structural changes. The first is the development of a hole in the ozone layer over the Antarctic, first discovered by British scientists in 1985. Since then a large area of ozone depletion over the Arctic and Northern Europe has been discovered. The second is the so-called "greenhouse effect". In addition there is the phenomenon of acid rain, which does not directly affect climatic structure, but which disastrously pollutes the atmosphere.

1. The Greenhouse Effect Threat

The "Greenhouse Effect" is the term now applied to the threat of the sudden heating up of the Earth's atmosphere through the excessive discharge into it of certain gases. These gases create a blanket which, like glass in a greenhouse, lets the sun's rays through to the earth, but traps some of the heat that would otherwise be radiated back into space. Since the last Ice Age the Earth's temperature has maintained a comfortable level of an average of about 15 degrees Celsius, warming at the rate of one C per 1000 years at the most. When it was 2 to 2.5 degrees warmer, some 70,000 years ago, elephants, lions, and hippopotami roamed Northern Europe. Scientists estimate that these gases have already warmed the Earth by 0.7 degrees C over the last 100 years and that, if this process continues unchecked, it is likely to add another 1.0 to 5.0 degrees C during the 21st century. The "best guess" is that the world could become 1 per cent warmer on the absolute scale of temperature by 2030.

This is beyond civilized man's experience. The world has not been as much as three degrees warmer than today for some two million years. This could just be the start. Less than 100 years from now, if present trends continue, the Earth could be a massive 8.6 degrees warmer. As a result of this heating up, the polar icecaps are expected to melt; sea levels will then rise, flooding low-lying areas such as Britain, Eastern America, Bangladesh and Egypt, and submerging many islands. Hurricanes will be more frequent and intense and the great food-producing plains of America and Russia will become arid. Their grain belts may move north to Canada and to the northern Russia, resulting in a net loss of food-producing capacity for the US. These changes are likely to be so rapid that living organisms will be unable to adjust to them. Signs of these phenomena are already appearing. The World Watch Institute in Washington estimates that one million square km could be at risk, involving a third of global cropland and a billion people. "Environmental refugees" are likely to be a phenomenon of the 21st century.

It is generally agreed that carbon dioxide accounts for roughly half of the global warming. Some 50 per cent of the carbon dioxide comes from the burning of fossil fuels, especially coal. The other 50 per cent from the burning down of the tropical forests – partly because burning releases carbon-dioxide, and partly because the leaves of trees absorb it. In Europe one 100-year-old beech tree purifies the air content of 800 homes annually. CFC (chloro-fluoro-carbon) gases account for a further 15-20% of the greenhouse effect; each molecule of the gases traps as much heat as 15,000 molecules of carbon dioxide. The other greenhouse gases include nitrous oxides given off by fertilizers and methane emanating from rubbish sites, paddy fields and animal excreta.

2. *The Ozone Threat*

Ozone, the three-atom form of oxygen, is the only gas in the atmosphere that limits the amount of harmful solar ultra-violet radiation reaching the earth. Increase of this radiation will promote skin cancers and cataracts, depress the human immune system, reduce crop yields and fish populations, damage some materials such as plastics, and increase smog. Continued ozone depletion will affect the well-being of every person on the planet.

Scientists are agreed that the ozone hole has been caused by CFCs and halons released into the atmosphere by the use of refrigerators, hamburger cartons, paint and hair sprays and fire extinguishers. These gases rise into the stratosphere where they literally devour ozone molecules. One molecule of chlorine can destroy 100,000 molecules of ozone.

3. *The Acid Rain Threat*

A third type of atmospheric pollutant, which, unlike CFCs and carbon dioxide, does not directly affect the climate, but which calls for urgent international action, is acid rain. This phenomenon occurs when sulphur and nitrogen oxides, emitted by coal-fired power stations, heavy industry factories and motor vehicles, undergo chemical changes in the atmosphere and fall as sulphuric and nitric acid, a "deadly cocktail", in rain, mist and snow. For some twenty five years acid rain has been falling on industrial Europe, West and East, and on North America. The cumulative effects are now apparent in the death of forests and their birds, of the fish and plants in lakes, rivers and coastal waters, in the poisoning of soil and ground water supplies, and the erosion of the fabric of marvellous ancient buildings, temples, cathedrals and so on.

If acid rain is unchecked, almost all the forests of Germany, Austria and Switzerland may be dead by the end of the century. Britain is the worst European polluter. The prevailing west winds blow its hideous effluents over Northern Europe, while the fresh sea of the Atlantic cleanses its own atmosphere. Half of Canada's acid rain comes from the US, and 15 to 25% of the US's acid rain comes from Canada. And uncontrolled industrialization is now producing acid rain in the developing countries. In India it is eroding the structure of the Taj Mahal.

C. Present Response to the Climatic Threat

1. Response to the Acid Rain Threat

Acid rain is controllable at source. Ninety five per cent of the emissions of sulphur dioxide and nitrogen oxides can be eliminated by technical adjustments to motor vehicles and coal-fired power stations and factories.

In West Europe, after much research into the problem – over 3000 studies had been made by 1984 – international action was initiated by the signing, in 1979, by 33 countries, of the Convention on Long-Range Transboundary Air Pollution. This treaty, negotiated by the United Nations Economic Commission for Europe (UNECE) – which, oddly enough, includes the US and Canada and did include the former USSR – provides the framework for protocols on different forms of pollution, which constitute binding commitments by the signatories to deal with the specified problems.

In 1984, under the auspices of the UNECE, ten countries formed the "Club of 30", committing themselves in a protocol to a 30 percent reduction of sulphur emissions from factories and power stations over the next ten years. They included the former USSR but not the US nor the UK. In 1988 this was complemented by a similar UNECE protocol under which 24 countries, including the US, the former USSR and the UK, committed themselves to freezing nitrogen oxide emissions from factories and power stations at the 1987 level by 1994. At the same time 12 West European countries – six of which are not members of the European Community – decided to go further, and in the Sofia Declaration announced that they would reduce their nitrogen oxide emissions by 30% by 1998. The national governments which have made these commitments are, of course, alone responsible for enforcing them.

Meanwhile the European Community has taken up the acid rain cause. In 1988, after long negotiations, it issued two directives. The first requires the 12 member states to reduce their sulphur and nitrogen oxide emissions from factories and power stations by certain percentages, different for each country, by 2003. The second lays down standards for vehicle emissions of these gases – but at levels four times as high as those established in the US. However, in April 1989 the European Parliament voted by a big majority to bring small car emissions down to the level of those of the US. In North America, Canada has undertaken, under a national acid rain control plan, to cut its sulphur emissions by half by 1994 and to place a permanent cap on the emissions. In an agreement of March 1991, the US and Canada agreed to a permanent reduction and stopping of these emissions. Like Canada, the US has imposed tough controls on vehicle emissions, but these are offset by the relentless increase in car traffic. Reduction in the numbers of motor vehicles in Europe as well as in North America must be regarded as an essential feature of acid rain control.

A beginning was therefore made in the 1980s in bringing acid rain under control through national an international legislation. But it seems clear that unless this legislative structure is greatly and quickly strengthened, it will not be successful. The lovely cover of living organisms which enfolds Europe and North America may be damaged beyond repair. Uniform, enforceable law is needed for the whole region. The basis exists. European Community law is enforced through its Court of Justice, to which individual European citizens have the right of appeal. And European Community law takes precedence over national law. What is urgently required is to extend this system to the whole UNECE region, comprising all of East and West Europe and North America, and ultimately to the whole world.

2. Response to the Ozone Threat

The halting of CFC emissions is at present a task for the industrialized countries, which are responsible for 90% of the ozone layer damage. It is essentially a straightforward matter, involving the creation of alternative synthetic chemicals for CFC's. These are now being produced, notably by the giant Du Pont chemical corporation in the US, which controls 25 per cent of the global market, and which plans to soon stop producing CFCs. The Director-General of UNEP estimates that such substitutes will reduce the greenhouse effect of CFCs (15 to 20 per cent of the total greenhouse effect) by 80 per cent.

It is encouraging that awareness of the ozone threat, first discovered in 1985, should have provoked almost immediate international action. The first global climate treaty, signed in Vienna in 1986, is a general agreement to tackle the ozone problem. The Montreal Protocol to this treaty is a specific commitment to action. This protocol, signed in September 1987, came into force on January 1st 1989 after being ratified by 28 governments, including the US, the former USSR, the European Community and Japan. Its signatories commit themselves to reduce their CFC emissions to 50% of their 1986 level by 1999. There is no provision for international enforcement.

By the end of 1988, however, two problems were apparent. First, new evidence emerged of a hole in the ozone layer over the Arctic Pole as well as over the Antarctic; and of the overall magnitude of the world's ozone loss, producing a strong scientific case to change the terms of the Treaty from a reduction to a complete elimination of CFCs. And to be effective, the Treaty must be universal. The developing countries see refrigeration as essential to a decent life-style for their peoples in the 21st century. They are not prepared to forego CFC production and/or imports unless the industrialized countries will help them by promoting the transfer of technology to make the substitute chemicals, and by some funding for this purpose. China and India, with a third of the world's population, are now starting to make CFCs themselves. The parties to the Protocol commit themselves, under Articles 9 and 10, to give technical assistance to the developing countries. But Dupont has refused to reveal its technology, and, according to Indian experts: "such a thing" as the transfer of technology "has never yet happened in the world".

These problems led to the renegotiation of the Protocol in London in June 1990. Eighty-one countries, including the US and those of the European Community, committed themselves to stop the production and consumption of CFCs and halon gases by the year 2000, and to review the Protocol in 1992. The EC countries together with Canada, Australia and New Zealand have advanced the date to 1997. It was also agreed – most reluctantly by the US — to establish a Global Environmental Fund, to which the rich countries would contribute to help the poor countries develop ozone-friendly technology. The US and other industrialized countries wanted this Fund to be under the aegis of the World Bank, which has set up a $1.5 billion Global Environment Facility (GEF), together with the United Nations Development Program (UNDP) and the United Nations Environment Program (UNEP). But the developing countries have insisted that it should be a separate fund over which they will have some effective control. It amounts only to $ 160 million for a period of three years, with an extra $ 80 million each to be added when India and China sign the Protocol. This China has now done, but not yet India, who still feels that there is too much Western control over the 14-member Council in charge of the Fund. The importance of securing the participation of these major developing countries in the implementation of the Protocol cannot be over-emphasized. The averting of the ozone-depletion threat depends as much on their desisting from buying or making CFCs as on the industrialized countries' abolition of the substances.

3. Response to the Greenhouse Effect Threat

The reduction of emissions of carbon dioxide into the air is an entirely different kind of problem from that of halting emissions of CFC's. It is impossible to burn wood or fossil fuels without releasing carbon dioxide, and it is impossible to control or reduce this gas once it has been released into the air. There is, therefore, only one solution: to halt or limit the burning of coal and wood. This involves fundamental changes in (a) tropical forest policies, and (b) world energy policies.

(a) Tropical Forest Policies

First we must note that the problem of deforestation links the climatic threat with every other aspect of the environmental threat in every part of the world. Without the trees, there is massive soil erosion leading often to floods. The forests contain wood for energy, on which a 1.3 per cent of the world's population at present depends, and plants and animals for food. And perhaps most crucial of all, the tropical forests contain 70 to 90 per cent of the world's millions of living species. Many species are as yet undiscovered and many will now never be discovered, vanishing forever with the trees. The human race's future diet – and its future source of medicines – will be foreclosed. Today, our diet is extremely limited: 90% of our plant food is derived from a mere 20 species. But experts estimate that 80,000 of the existing 300,000 plant species have the potential to produce food for human consumption. Genetic engineering offers hope of adequate food for the 10 billion people who will soon be living on the planet – if the forest's gene bank is preserved. Commercial sales of drugs based on tropical forest's plants are estimated at nearly $ 30 billion a year. Meanwhile, the threatened climatic warming will itself add to the destruction of the gene bank, since many species will probably be unable to adapt to the new temperatures.

The world's tropical forests are situated mainly in Central and South America (over half the total), Central and West Africa (a fifth of the total), and South East Asia (a quarter of the total). A third of the forests are in Brazil.

It is estimated that, since 1900, the tropical rain forests have been reduced by 40 percent, and that, at present rates of deforestation – 50 acres per minute globally – by the end of the century the forests of Latin America will be reduced by a further 40 percent and those of South East Asia and West Africa will have virtually disappeared.

In practical terms, the solution to the forest problem seems fairly straightforward. It involves:

1. The halting of tree cutting;
2. The planting of new trees. The World Watch Institute in Washington, D.C. estimates that a total of 130 million hectares in developing countries needs to be planted with 15 billion trees during the next 15 years, together with 40 million hectares in the industrialized countries;
3. The pursuit of policies of "sustainable utilization" of forest products – timber, food and genetic species.

These policies will require substantial investment, and need to be supported by thorough scientific research – very little is being done at present. They call for enforceable codes of practice to be observed by peasants, farmers, industrialists, national governments and multinationals.

In today's world, national governments and their citizens will obviously be the main agents for carrying out such policies. But since the forests stretch across frontiers, regional co-operation will be essential. And since the forests crucially affect the global climate, and provide resources essential to human life everywhere, there is a global interest in their maintenance and care.

In the late 1980s the governments of most of the tropical forest countries, confronted by the frightening results of forests destruction and prodded by Western environmentalists, had begun to wake up to the need for action. In October 1988 President Sarney of Brazil, after hearing of 6000 Amazon fires burning in one day, decided to reverse two decades of government encouragement of "the conquest of the jungles". He halted tax breaks and other government incentives to promote forest clearing and banned log exports. But he has not increased government funding for environmental protection. There are fewer than 1000 officers to enforce the new rules in an area larger than that of Western Europe. The Brazilian military, who stand in the shadow behind the President and who are hand in glove with the great landlords and foreign companies who are cutting down the forests, are raising the cry that environmentalism is a foreign plot to subvert Brazilian sovereignty.

India's national forest policy, introduced in 1952 as part of its overall economic plan, gave priority to the production of industrial forest products. In the face of massive deforestation Prime Minister Gandhi reversed this policy. He assigned forestry a central place in the Plan for 1985-90, tripled its funding and involved villagers and tribesmen in forest conservation – a "peoples' movement for afforestation". The new policy aims at recovering 12 million acres a year for fuel wood and fodder plantations.

In Malaysia and Thailand laws have been recently made to control or forbid commercial logging. Sri Lanka has employed a Finnish firm to draw up a Forest Master Plan. Nepal is drawing up a *Master Plan for the Forestry Sector*, for which 30% of the funds will be sought overseas.

The Chinese Government identified the forest problem sooner; between 1948 and 1978 it organized the planting of 28 million hectares with trees, increasing national forest cover from 9 to 13%. After a decline between 1979 and 1985, tree planting surged forward when the peasants were given the right to own the trees they plant, to use the land planted for 30-50 years, and to bequeath it.

The World Watch Institute in Washington believes that the Chinese Government's target of 20% forest cover by the year 2000 may be achieved. But it seems certain that the rest of the developing world's forest countries will not be able to halt the progress of destruction without the transfer of funds, technology and other forms of help from the North.

International bodies, like national governments, have failed, until very recently, to focus on the need for positive forestry polices. "From 1980 through 1984, the major development banks allocated less than one per cent of their annual financing to forestry, and the UN Development Programme (UNDP) only 2 per cent", writes the World Watch Institute.

At the international level, a *Tropical Forestry Action Plan* was launched in 1985 by the FAO, UNDP, the World Bank and the Washington-based World Resources Institute. It calls for the investment of 8 billion dollars over five years in tree planting projects and efforts to arrest deforestation.

"It is conceived as a pattern of guidelines which should be adopted by those working on forest projects at all levels and in all countries. A key ingredient is active participation by millions of small farmers and landless people who daily use forests and trees to meet their needs."

The key to its success will obviously be adequate funding and monitoring. Meanwhile the World Bank and other development banks have begun to write environmental protection criteria into their loans, and to suspend funds if these are not implemented.

These small United Nations' activities are supplemented by a small independent body, the International Tropical Timber Organization (ITTO), set up in 1985 by 41 states. Its main supporters are the principal consumers – Japan, the European Community and the US. Its purpose is to promote "the sustainable utilization and conservation of tropical forests and their genetic resources". It has made a beginning by committing $1 million of its tiny budget of $4 million (in 1988) to a project to ascertain the "sustainable productivity" of logging in the Brazilian State of Acre, which could become a model for other projects. Little can be achieved, however, without a change in international trade policies and corporate attitudes. The tropical timber trade amounts at present to about $6 billion a year; yet the international firms concerned have not yet contributed a cent to the ITTO.

Meanwhile prices of tropical timber in world markets are low, so that the producer states cannot earn enough revenues from timber exports to pay for reafforestation and forest management. ITTO's small staff lacks even one expert to advise exporting states on production sustainability.

Non-Governmental Organizations such as the World-Wide Fund for Nature (WWF) are working with national governments on projects such as the organization of national parks in the tropical forests.

To sum up: national governments and international organizations are only just awakening to the need for urgent action to save the world's tropical forests. Some small steps have been taken, but they are miniscule in relation to the huge threat. It will be necessary to mobilize governments, landlords, multinational companies, small entrepreneurs, peasants and tribesmen in a co-operative effort to preserve existing forests and plant new trees. And it will be essential to relate such forestry policies to policies which provide alternative energy sources for the two billion people who at present derive their energy needs from wood. Some hard battles may have to be fought.

(b) Energy Policies

The problem of halting the burning of coal is of a different order from that of reviving the forests. The fossil-fuels, coal and oil, have for the past 200 years provided the energy which has powered the industrial revolution. But oil reserves are becoming exhausted – they may last 40 to 50 years; and now coal burning threatens the climate. The fossil fuel era is inexorably ending; in the next century humankind will have to look to other forms of energy. The industrialized countries, which with a quarter of the world's population emit three quarters of the fossil-fuel-generated carbon dioxide, will have to make a major effort to renounce coal by conserving energy and seeking alternative sources. The developing countries, launching into industrialization, are challenged to jump straight from wood into the post fossil-fuel era. If they turn to coal, "in 20 years' time," warns Dr. Jose Goldenberg, one of Brazil's top energy experts, "the developing countries will be the main producers of carbon dioxide", which means that the industrial countries are challenged in their own interests to help the developing countries to launch into new forms of energy.

The problem of meeting the energy needs of the world's exploding population in the 21st century is therefore both complex and intractable. This is not the place to launch into a discussion of post-fossil fuel energy options. Suffice it to note that fission nuclear power presents hazards of a kind which humanity has never before experienced. A number of countries have deliberately renounced it, in some cases after plebiscites. They include Sweden, Austria, Australia, New Zealand, Norway, Ireland, Greece, Italy, Denmark, Portugal, Luxembourg, and the Philippines. The Austrian Foreign Minister told the 1986 meeting of the International Atomic Energy Agency (IAEA) that:

"For us the lessons of Chernobyl are clear. The Faustian bargain of nuclear energy has been lost. It is high time to leave the path of nuclear energy, to develop new alternatives and clean sources of energy . . . . This is the price to enable life to continue on this planet."

On the other hand, proponents of nuclear energy, who are at present dominant in Britain, Japan, France and West Germany, and vocal in the US, argue that there is no practical alternative to fill the looming energy gap. "Renewables", energy from wind, water and sunlight, cannot, they say, meet the needs of a modern industrial society. The Brundtland Report of 1987 opts for a "low energy future", grounded on conservation and the development of "new and renewable sources" as the only realistic option open to the world for the 21st century.

The problems of storing high-level radio-active waste and of disposing of spent reactors, whose span is about thirty years are intractable. Not one in the world has yet been dismantled. Meanwhile the two great developing countries which contain a third of the world's population, China and India, are going ahead with industrialization on the basis of coal and nuclear energy. In 1989 India had 14 reactors operative or under construction, and China 3 under construction . (Comparable figures for countries in the industrialized world are: France: 64; Britain: 42; Germany: 36; former Soviet Union: 79; US: 104; Canada: 22). China's Energy Plan for the 1990s provides for the production of 1.4 billion tons of coal; and India has vast run reserves.

Four conclusions concerning energy policy emerge:

1. Decisions on energy policy taken now will profoundly affect future generations;

2. It has become senseless for energy policy to be decided on a purely national basis;

3. The technological problems involved in energy choices are so far-reaching that it is essential that the scientific brain power and research funds of the world should be concentrated on them;

4. In the next century the marriage of high technology to renewables may solve the energy problem, and the developing countries, leap-frogging the fossil fuel era, may get there first. Already India is spending nearly a billion dollars on solar cell technology. American scientists in New Mexico have recently produced a multi-layer solar cell which could lead to large solar energy conversion systems in sunny parts of the world. This would be economically competitive for energy utilities.

Another break-through in solar cell energy is occurring in Japan. Yukinori Kuwano, founder of the company Sanyo Electric, calculates that "world energy needs in 2000 could be met by just 836.6 square kilometres (323 square miles) of solar panels covering a mere four per cent of its deserts. Superconductor cables would carry the power to regions with less sunlight . . ." the power of the "amorphous silicon solar cells" which his company is producing could, he calculates, "provide the energy equivalent of 3.65 billion gallons of oil, or the anticipated annual consumption of oil, coal, hydropower and all other primary energy sources". At present solar power is four or five times as expensive as the other kinds of power which are now plentiful. But its price is steadily falling. And would it not be in humanity's interest to divert a trillion dollars a year from lethal arms to benign energy? Fusion energy – the harnessing of the energy equivalent of a hydrogen bomb for peaceful purposes – is another possible source of benign energy; its raw material would be sea water and there would be very little radio-active waste. But so far, after many years of research in Europe and the US, the technological break-through has not been achieved.

In the face of what may be regarded as a crying need for the "globalization" of energy – global research, global planning, global law and global management – there is at present no United Nations Specialized Agency for Energy. The functions of the 112-member state International Atomic Energy Agency in Vienna (IAEA) are limited to the promotion of peaceful nuclear power and the monitoring of its military use in connection with the Nuclear Non-Proliferation Treaty. It has not even negotiated internationally acceptable radiation standards.

(c) Response to the Greenhouse Effect Threat at the International Level

In the late 1980s awareness of the catastrophic proportions of the greenhouse effect in some circles was one of near panic; conferences were held, research projects set up and proposals proliferated. A summit meeting of 24 national leaders held at The Hague in March 1989, and speeches made by Mr. Shevardnadze and Mr. Gorbachev at the General Assembly of the UN in 1988, called for the establishment of an organ of the United Nations to be given effective powers to administer and manage environmental policy (UNEP has no such powers). Mr. Shevardnadze proposed "an Environmental Council capable of taking effective decisions to ensure ecological security", and the

Declaration of the Hague called for "developing, within the framework of the United Nations, a new institutional authority, either by strengthening existing institutions or by creating a new institution, which in the context of the preservation of the earth's atmosphere, shall be responsible for combating any further global warming of the atmosphere", and which will take decisions by *majority vote* (my emphasis).

Mr. Gorbachev proposed the creation of "an international space laboratory exclusively for monitoring the state of the environment". And monitoring implies enforcement.

The Prime Ministers of France, The Netherlands and Norway who convened the Hague Summit, informally floated a more radical proposal: the creation of a special body, to be called GLOBE, which would lay down and monitor world pollution standards and enforce them by economic sanctions.

M. Mitterand, the French President, said at a press conference after the Hague Summit that the establishment of "an international environmental authority" would involve the renunciation of "some sovereignty" by every country. "We have in essence empowered the European Community to take decisions in many environmental fields", he declared. "We French are naturally prepared to do at the world level what we have done in the European framework."

The Maltese Foreign Minister, Mr. Vincent Tabone, proposed in the General Assembly that the doctrine of "the common heritage of mankind" should be applied to the climate. It will be recalled that the Common Heritage doctrine was first put forward by Malta in 1970 with reference to the minerals in the deep oceans, and subsequently written into the Law of the Sea Treaty. The minerals in the oceans belong to no-one, so it is fairly straightforward to declare that they belong to everyone. But the climate is a different matter. As we have seen, it is conditioned by fossil fuel burning, the chemical emissions of modern machines and the chemistry of trees. Are these assets to belong to everyone? The implications for vesting the United Nations and its related organs with rights and powers to own, manage and control "property" and basic "commons" are profound. World management implies world government.

Policies will depend, of course, on the "political will" of national leaders. But something new is happening to influence this will: a vast groundswell of energy and concern at the grassroots level. In the industrialized world this is expressed in the rapid proliferation of environmental and Green groups, in both the Western and the communist countries.

In the developing countries, peasants, tribesmen and women are emerging from their traditional social ruts to act locally to organize their own development, including the protection of their forests. Women are hugging trees in India to prevent their felling (the Chipko Movement); women are planting trees in Kenya (the Green Belt Movement); and trade unionists, such as Chico Mendes, are dying in Brazil to save the trees. Much of this activity is linked up with environment and development groups in the Western world. (See the Club of Rome's Report of 1988, *The Barefoot Revolution*.) And now, suddenly, a grass-roots gesture has dramatized the plight of the forests to the whole world. In February 1989, the Indians of the Altimara region in Brazil organized an inter-tribal "Summit" to protest the planned construction of an enormous dam on the mighty Xingu River which would flood a huge area for the production of electricity. Two hundred media persons and 100 international observers, including a British Member of Parliament (Tam Dalyel) and a member of the European Parliament (Paul Staes) turned up for this "event" which was publicized to the whole world. The World Bank and the US Government have suspended their loans for the dam. And the humble rubber-tapper Chico Mendes, victim of murder by landlords' hired thugs – a regular Amazonian occurrence – has become an international martyr. "Brazil is back to normal" writes a British journalist (Walter Schwartz) who was at Altimara, "but the ecological movement has been changed for all time".

This grass-roots energy needs to be channeled into the global environment strategy. The new forest policies of the Indian and

Chinese Governments, noted above, and the policies of FAO's Tropical Forests Action Plan and of the International Tropical Timber Organization (ITTO) recognize the importance of listening to and working with the grass-roots people. If this process is not rapidly developed on a wide front, a dangerous confrontational situation is likely to arise. "Because self-reliant localism cannot tackle the broader issues of resource distribution, legal rights and ecological decline, many self-help movements have turned increasingly to political struggle, bringing them more into line with industrial-country environmental groups that have long operated by political means", writes the World-Watch Institute in an important new study of world-wide grass-roots action. In other words, governments, military, landlords and corporations will find themselves increasingly confronted by millions of enraged and desperate peasants – men and women.

In 1991 the process began of drawing together these and many other threads in preparation for the United Nations Conference on Environment and Development (UNCED), a Summit conference of at least 100 world leaders to be held in Brazil in June 1992, which some believe could mark a turning point in world history. If it fails in the 21st century, the whole world could sink in the 21st century, into economic collapse and environmental disaster. If it succeeds, the basis for a new world order could be laid on a higher level of morality and happiness than the world has ever known.

The Conference plans to produce:

1. An "Earth charter"of basic principles for the conduct of people and nations with respect to environment and development;

2. Draft Conventions (i.e. treaties) concerning the atmosphere, biodiversity, forests, and the use and abuse of the climate in war;

3. "Agenda 21", an agreed work program for the international community, setting forth targets, cost estimates, modalities and assignments of responsibilities;

4. Plans for new and additional funding resources for these policies;

5. Plans for the transfer of technology;

6. The strengthening of the needed institutional structures and processes.

These policies and documents have been discussed at a series of "PrepComs" held in Geneva; a final PrepCom will be held in New York in March before the Conference takes place in Rio in June 1992. None of the PrepCom documents have yet been finalized, and I have not seen any of the drafts. Press reports so far are discouraging. But this is not surprising. For underlying the Conference Agenda is the fundamental issue facing the world today. It has been well stated by Martin Khor of the NGO Third World Network:

> "It is as though the conference is saying that the best way to solve the global environmental and economic problems caused by 20 per cent of the world's population who consume 80 per cent of the world's resources is to promote sustainable development in the South".

(The head of the US delegation to the Geneva PrepCom in September, 1991, described proposals for the conservation of energy and the possibility of an energy tax as a potential violation of national sovereignty). The true solution has been summed up by a British clergyman, Canon Dammers: "Live simply, that others may simply live".

The key criteria for the success or failure of the Conference will surely be: (i) Whether massive transfer of funds and technology from the rich to the poor, including the cancellation of $1.3 trillion in debt, is agreed; and (ii) Whether effective international institutions for formulating, carrying out and enforcing global environmental and development policies are agreed. The Resolution passed by the World Federalist Council in July 1991 on this subject is attached as Appendix A.

The world's fundamental moral issue, the vast gulf between rich and poor outlined at the beginning of this essay, has been on the international agenda for 30 years – and the gulf has widened. But for the first time the poor have major clout. On their co-operation in the Rio program depends the survival of us all; and this co-operation will not be forthcoming unless the rich begin to think in terms of living simply, reducing consumerism, replacing competition by co-operation, and profits by sharing and caring. Sources used: Worldwatch Institute, Washington; The Guardian and The Observer newspapers, London; Development Forum (a UN journal); Friends of the Earth, UK; Greenpeace, UK; the Environmental Digest (a British journal); Exchange (the journal of the National Wildlife Federation, USA); the journal of the Rocky Mountain Institute, USA; literature from the Woods Hole Research Center, Massachusetts; UNEP's monthly Newsletter; European Community booklet on Environment; World-Wide Fund for Nature (WWF), UK; *Acid Rain* by Steven Elsworth, (Pluto Press, 1984).

Appendix A.

Resolution of the World Federalist Movement on Environment Policy

1) Recognizing that remedies to global environment problems require: a) real limitations of national sovereignty, and b) transfers of technology and financial resources from wealthy to less wealthy nations, involving a global taxation system; and

2) Referring to the proposal of the Expert Group of the World Commission of Experts on Environment and Development (The Brundtland Commission) of 1986 that states shall "justly establish or resort to an institutional mechanism or other appropriate arrangement," and to the Hague Declaration on protection of the atmosphere which calls for a world environmental   authority with delegation of national sovereignty on the environment and with binding majority decision-making and decisions enforceable through international courts;

The World Federalist Movement adopts the *Proposal for a General UN System for Protection of the Environment*, submitted by the Commission of

Experts, on the establishment and implementation of binding international regulations. This proposal:

1) calls for a general international convention to cover all threats to the environment that require international action and to provide coordination through a common system for the combat of the various threats, including those which are covered by special conventions lacking adequate provisions for adoption and execution of the necessary measures;

2) should form a substantial part of World Federalist Movement's contribution to the UN conference on Environmental and Development (UNCED), to be supplemented by World Federalist Movement proposals discussing economic development issues;

The convention shall notably provide for a regime for:

1) Adoption of binding international regulations by a plenary organ (the UN General Assembly or a special environmental assembly) by a qualified majority vote not allowing a single state veto;

2) Directly applicable regulations for the high seas, outer space and through the Antarctic Treaty Organization, for Antarctica;

3) Surveillance and control of threats to the environment generally and of execution in the several states of international environmental law laid down in treaties and regulations;

4) Sanctions against violators of the obligations;

5) Compulsory jurisdiction in relevant disputes for the International Court of Justice, or if its stature cannot be amended to admit international organizations as parties to disputes, for a special environmental court;

6) A system for international financing of important measures in favour of promoting the sustainable development of less wealthy countries based upon general levies, or upon special levies on activities which are detrimental to the environment, e.g. burning of fossil fuels;

7) The necessary institutions including an environmental Council, with Permanent seats for the major states, monitored by a Parliamentary Assembly, and with equal representation of industrialized and developing countries, to prepare and execute the regulations.

Adopted in The Netherlands, 26 July 1991 at the XII Congress of the World Federalist Movement

The Three Revolutions of Homo Sapiens

DIGBY MCLAREN*

The First Revolution

Homo sapiens has been around for over forty or fifty thousand years, perhaps as long as one hundred thousand. During that time, beings with today's cranial capacity and, presumably, intelligence have inhabited different regions of the planet, with earlier populations that probably never rose above a few hundreds of thousands in total. Food and waste, therefore, were plainly not a problem to our early ancestors. But about three hundred generations ago (9 or 10 thousand years), a slow but major change took place. This was the agricultural revolution, when we began to plant seed and harvest crops, and to domesticate animals for food and power. The confrontation of the farmers and the cowboys goes back that far. As soon as we could produce surplus food, job specialization increased the rate of technological development and it was found convenient to live in one place and organize food supply from the surrounding countryside. This led to an increase in population, although in each of the independent regions of the world where such developments were taking place, very large fluctuations in population were the norm. These were due to unexpected climate change, epidemics, wars, migrations, and, in some instances, collapse of farming systems from injudicious overuse of soil or irrigation. The whole human machine was fuelled by the sun. We ate plants and animals and used animals, and almost universally, slaves, for transport and agricultural work.

---

* From the Symposium "Our Environment/Our Health", Radisson Hotel, Ottawa, November 11-13, 1990, Opening Plenary Session

Waste was produced, but was largely self cleansing and there was no long-term depletion of energy resources because they all sprang from the sun. Certainly some hazardous wastes were produced, perhaps the most dangerous being the toxic chemicals in smoke from wood fires and the poisoning of soils resulting from injudicious irrigation. Earth resource use was limited to building materials, ceramics, native metals such as tin and copper and, about five thousand years ago, we learned how to smelt iron with charcoal and to make glass. Technology certainly advanced, but not the quantity of the energy source. By the Middle Ages many men and women were well clothed, could travel widely on foot or in horse-drawn carriages or on horseback. They ate abundant meats and vegetables and lit their homes with animal or vegetable oils and waxes. Wastes were still self-cleansing for the most part, although cities, from Rome onwards, were extremely unhealthy places to live, and massive plagues swept across many parts of the world, changing the demographic patterns drastically from time to time. By the mid 18th century improved agricultural practices and the beginning of improvements in hygiene led to a slow increase in population. Throughout the whole of the time since the agricultural revolution, the system functioned on energy from the sun, but at a rate that was strictly limited. This allowed the population to grow up to, say, half a billion at the most without unduly straining the resources base, or the ecosphere.

The Second Revolution

Another revolution was in the offing. It is an irony of history that Malthus lived at the end of the 18th Century and wrote his famous essay contrasting geometric growth of population with arithmetic growth of food production. The Industrial Revolution quickly showed him to be wrong – but only for two hundred years, as we shall see. The revolution was based on a complete reversal of the energy system up to that point. Humans discovered how to use fossil fuels in a big way: coal, including brown coal and peat; oil, including heavy oils and tar sands; and natural gas. This was a big breakthrough and we made the Faustian bargain under which the rate of energy supply to support life was no longer restricted largely to photosynthesis by plants, but became seemingly infinite by using past solar energy, stored, over a period of about 400 million years, within the earth's crust. The other side of the bargain, however, was that the quantity of power stored in fossil fuels is in fact finite; and some time in the future we shall run out. We shall have a look later at how soon that will be. There are, furthermore, other serious drawbacks to the use of fossil fuels.

Starting with coal, we made machines which gave us the capacity to mine deep within the ground and to bring out more coal and minerals, enabling us to build steam engines and pumps and to power new ways of travelling on wheels and in boats. This also, ironically, freed us from dependence on plants, animals and slaves for energy. Machines and fertilizers changed agriculture and freed surplus labour from the land. We built factories, increased the size of cities and there was food for all. Only one thing wrong. In the early part of the 19th century the major cities of the world were subject to outbreaks of cholera every four or five years and it appeared that the city provided an ideal environment for the plague to spread. This kept the population down a little longer in spite of the cornucopia released by technology.

The countries of the world began to do something about it. For example, in Britain, Sir Edwin Chadwick, a distinguished physician and activist was given the task of examining the problems of city health and advising the Poor-Law Commission on what should be done. He made a survey across Britain and produced a brilliant report in 1848 recommending simple but revolutionary measures: burial of the dead according to certain standards, a clean water tap at the end of every street, disposal of sewage underground rather than in open ditches in the street, and certain housing standards in regards to availability of fresh air and sunshine. By 1849 the Private Enterprise Society was formed in London to fight against the new regulations. But cholera was a persuasive advocate and the landlords did not prevail. Little by little hygiene laws were introduced and their effects were electric.

There was now no further restraint on population growth, and for the first time in the whole of history human beings looked forward to a major increase in expectation of life. By the mid 19th Century, also for the first time in history, the population reached one billion, and then at an increasing rate, it began to grow. Every 20 years from 1890 to 1990 the population increased in billions in the following manner: 1.5, 1.7, 2, 2.5, 3.6, 5.3 in 1990. Plot them on a curve and see what it looks like and then extrapolate for the next 20 years. Malthus has truly come home to roost. However, we find that energy use has grown even faster. Considering only the fossil fuels, and measured in terawatts (1 terawatt is equivalent to burning 1 billion tonnes of coal or 5 billion barrels of oil per year), we find that the cumulative usage total since 1850 was about 10 in 1890 , and once again, going up every 20 years, it increased to: 26, 54, 97, 196, 393 in 1990. This represents a doubling every 20 years.

So we've produced two mega-problems in the last two hundred years:

1. We have a population of 5.3 billion growing rapidly;
2. We have used one fifth of the total energy endowment of oil and gas.

If the present level of increase continues, we shall have used 80% of the recoverable endowment within the next 30 or 40 years. By that time we might have serious warming and a huge increase in toxic wastes.

At this point I would like to introduce economics, although in a great deal of what I have been saying economics are implicitly involved. How do our present economic systems appear in the light of what we are finding out about this crisis situation currently facing us? Do they reflect values, instincts and institutional structures that inhibit reform of human behaviour towards survivability? In 1971, Georgescu-Roegen introduced thermodynamics into economic theory. He pointed out that the natural dowry on earth consists of two distinct elements: the stock of materials with a high energy potential on or within the globe (low entropy) and the flow of solar energy. He claimed that the future depends on the relative importance of these two elements and that the entire stock of natural resources is not worth more than a few days of sunlight. We have seen how the start of the industrial revolution marked a fundamental change in the capacity of our race to dominate the environment – a change from the use of solar energy in plants and animals to energy from fossil fuels and mineral resources stored in the crust of the earth. Past economic thinking has been caught up in a system that assumed limitless resources and ignored production of waste. This worked when resources did appear to be limitless and waste was easily disposed of. Neither of these conditions exists any longer. The economic subsystem, as a way of organizing human behaviour, takes in resources and excretes waste, and is thus irrevocably and closely linked to the ecosystem. Input and output are finite and the main variable is the one-way flow of matter-energy. By looking at things this way, we can question how big the consumption of physical and biosphere resources should be in relation to the dimensions of the global system. This necessarily questions the concept of economic growth and the impossibility of generalizing western standards to the world as a whole. We know that one quarter of the population uses most of the resources and produces most of the waste; can we increase both in the other three quarters? What are the limits that must exist, as in every finite system? Have we passed those limits in terms of global sustainability, and particularly within our own privileged enclave?

I should like, briefly, to say something about the longer-term effects of the Industrial Revolution that are coming into prominence today owing to the massive population growth. The ecosystem, which is almost as old as the earth itself, has been adjusted to a solar energy system in support of life. Humans were also more or less in balance with the system until the agricultural revolution. Life, therefore, was adjusted to the chemical environment of the earth's surface including the atmosphere, hydrosphere and lithosphere. When we started digging into the earth to bring out new substances – all the fossil fuels, and many metallic ores – we added a new supply of chemicals to the surface environment, many of which are extremely poisonous and which have deleterious effects on all life. Because of the rate at which we are increasing the use of the fossil fuels, we are flooding our environment, the atmosphere and hydrosphere and the surface of the land, with much larger fluxes of metals and organic carbon compounds than it has ever had to face before, including the complex and dangerous molecules formed when we burn or even spill petroleum, as well as coal. This flux is increasing, and the effects are becoming increasingly visible and measurable. There are also the new chemicals which we are creating deliberately. These man-made compounds are also making their mark on the environment, and changing life on earth. Most dangerous of all these are probably the CFCs, and their effects in depleting the ozone layer are already measurable, not just in increased cancer risk in humans, but, more seriously, in stress symptoms in the primary food chain of plant microplankton in Antarctica.

So what do we do about all this and what is relevant to our concerns on environment and health? At this point I should like to refer to a paper by Dr. John Last and Dr. Tee L. Guidotti on *Implications for Human Health of Global Ecological Changes*. I was fortunate to receive a draft which was prepared for the Canadian Public Health Association and supported by a resolution at its annual meeting in June 1990. They comment on the demographic changes taking place in the world, and the terrible problems raised by what they term the "biological costs of human reproductive success." They plead for a need to emphasize issues that affect the entire planet and suggest that a new initiative should involve physicians and medical and health organizations in international concerns over environmental quality. They recognize that the "current disastrously wrong approach to planetary management is bad for human health as well as for the health of the earth". They make a plea that the actions of the International Physicians for the Prevention of Nuclear War be emulated and point out that they played a constructive role because they were able to inform public and health professionals about a problem in which the health dimension was not immediately obvious. They state that the world environment is rapidly approaching or is perceived to be approaching the same critical level of risk as nuclear war.

The Third Revolution

I should like to suggest that we are entering a third revolution. The effects of the Industrial Revolution have left us with no alternative but to attack two major problems that will require staggeringly large adjustments to our current system – globally. We have no choice but to stop and then reverse the population increase, and to reduce and then reverse the profligate use of fossil fuels if we are to end the current acceleration to disaster.

We are confronted with a moral dilemma that concerns the health of humanity and the health of the planet. We are faced with the paradox that actions we consider ethical and just must adversely affect the ecosphere and thus inevitably cause increased environmental degradation with further destruction of our own life-support system. I refer primarily to population and suggest that the only fully humane action we can take in the face of this dilemma is to attack immediately the horror of bringing babies into the world to die in their first year or to survive for a life dominated by malnutrition, disease and diminishing life expectancy. We should also realize that babies in Northern cultures will use resources and produce wastes many times more than the three quarters of the global population of the South. We must overcome the reluctance to recognize that it is not interference with the rights of a woman to offer to her advice and assistance regarding family planning and methods to achieve it.

Two hundred years ago all energy used by humankind was solar – through plants and animals. In two hundred years time the inhabitants of the earth will continue to exist only by using solar energy converted by a variety of systems, but in balance with the ecosphere. This implies a major reduction in population as well as in energy use. If this cannot be achieved, then all bets are off.

International Legislation on Environment

RUTH GUNNARSEN

"Think Globally and Act Locally" has long been the slogan used by people with an understanding for problems connected with the environment and the North-South question.

We, who live in industrialized countries, cannot postpone drastic changes in our lifestyle, since we allow our over-consumption to create under-development in the Third World. But we cannot expect all people to change their way of life and patterns of consumption voluntarily. This is why we will have to legislate.

In the future, those who possess the technology should no longer be the only ones who determine to what extent it can be used. For example, the right to undertake mining operations at great depth in the oceans should not be limited to a few nations or companies. Nor should only those countries who possess the necessary technology be allowed to exploit Antarctica. Fishing quotas should no longer depend on the size of the fishing fleets, but on the quantities of fish available. We must learn to redirect our technology to serve the interests of humankind as a whole. It is apparent that an all-embracing legislation must be insisted upon. Pollution knows no national boundaries; therefore, this legislation has to be on a supranational level, a kind of world authority.

Dealing with environmental issues must be clearly divided into legislative, executive and judicial functions. The legislators will have to approach the problems at a basic level. The fewest possible issues will have to be brought to superior courts. First of all, pollution and the abuse of environment will have to be stopped at the very source. The police and established legal procedures can be used once the new laws are introduced. Thereafter the responsibility for law enforcement will pass into the hands of the municipalities and provincial authorities, or whatever regional entities a country is divided into. In many cases these authorities will be able to act within the country's own legal framework. However, we cannot manage without also legislating on an international and supranational level. The legal term for this is *subsidiarity*, a blend of centralization and decentralization. At present, supranational legislation is imperative on the following issues:

1. The atmosphere, in order to put a stop to the greenhouse effect, ozone depletion and acid rain;
2. Antarctica;
3. International waters.

The channels available for individual complaints should be identical with the ones used by the supranational authorities which have created the rules.

Where to activate legislators to create better laws on environment?

The General Assembly of the UN has had environmental questions on its agenda and will be able to influence the general international development, but not to a large extent. The following institutions are within the framework of the UN:

1. UNEP (United Nations Environment Program), based in Nairobi, Kenya;
2. ICJ (International Court of Justice) in the Hague in Holland.

In addition there are regulations to come in regional courts, for example, the Council of Europe in Strasbourg and institutions of a different character, such as ministries of Education, Environment, Energy and Agriculture.

Information regarding the need for a cleaner environment has already produced results. In Denmark, for instance, the Ministry of Energy's action plan, which aims at an 80% reduction of sulphur-dioxide (SO_2) emissions by the year 2000, has already resulted in a 10% reduction. According to the General Council of the Danish Petrol Industry, this has been achieved with the help of new technology, energy saving, reorganization of energy consumption and a general demand for petrol containing a lower grade of sulphur. Information and common sense are, however, insufficient when they are confronted with economic interests that weigh heavily. We have for economic reasons opted for an increase of free trade, which might result in m o r e mismanagement of our resources and an intensified exploitation of the environment.

UNEP (United Nations Environment Program)

The greatest danger faced by international proposals and regulations concerning the environment is the danger of being ignored. Transgressors will hardly bother to act in accordance with rules that are not generally known and that cannot be enforced by any authority. UNEP, based in Nairobi, will have to be given the power to ensure that all nations include a section on the environment in their constitutions. The introduction of one of UNEP's motions on international legislation on the environment states: "Every manifestation of life is unique. The protection of the law must be extended to every living creature, regardless of its importance to others." (It is doubtful that this should be taken literally, to include even the microbes of tuberculosis and syphilis). All nations must, in accordance herewith, create a moral code that can be enforced, as well as plans of action. UNEP must be given the support to promote further research and information that will serve as background for future legislation.

The International Court of Justice

In 1989 the UN unanimously accepted a proposal by the non-aligned nations to proclaim the next ten years the Decade of International Law. The objective is to give the International

Court of Justice the authority that will enable it to function effectively as a UN institution.

The aims of this Decade of International Law are as stated below:

1. to promote respect for the principles of international law;
2. to instigate a progressive development of international law and its resulting systematization.

The hope is that the International Court of Justice in the Hague can celebrate its 100th anniversary at the turn of the century as a UN tribunal with all the powers of a tribunal at its disposal. The International Court of Justice has undergone many improvements since it was created but it is still far from comprehensive, and it is not functioning effectively enough. Many countries have not accepted it yet. Its jurisdiction is not compulsory, meaning that an accused country cannot be forced to appear in court. Neither can it prosecute individuals. And all its 15 judges have always been men. Many of the functions have to be modified before it will be able to be used as a creator and administrator of international justice. Nevertheless the International Court of Justice presents the best of existing possibilities. The UN could collapse like a house of cards. We can help to prevent that by increasing the capacity of the Court, which has already survived great difficulties. It was founded in 1899, at the first international peace conference (under a different name). It did not go down with the League of Nations after the First World War. It was later incorporated into the UN system.

Recently we have been witnessing a promising tendency of international co-operation to reinforce the UN as a supranational authority. A reinforcement of the International Court of Justice was decided upon during the first meeting of the non-aligned nations and a large number of NGO's (Non-Governmental Organizations) in Summer of 1990 in The Hague. One of them, the World Federalist Movement, was the initiator to gain the support to the non-aligned nations. The US was rather averse at the start of the discussion on the International Law Decade in the UN. No doubt, part of the reason was that international justice, meaning international law that can enforce its judgements, will render the concept of a great power or a superpower obsolete.

Laws concerning the atmosphere, outer space and the seas, as well as an internationalization of Antarctica are clearly areas for international legislation.

International Law of the Sea

Hugo Grotius was the first well-known person who proposed international legislation on the sea. He was born in Holland in 1583 and died in exile in 1645. His philosophical work "De Mare Liberum" concerns the right of all nations to sail freely on the open seas. We consider the seas even today as the mother of life on earth and an area which has to be regulated by international legislation. Already in the past this legislation ran into obstacles. All of Hugo Grotius' possessions were confiscated and he received a life sentence in Holland. He succeeded in escaping to several other countries in Europe, where he was able to write the book, which today is considered the fundamental book on international law, *De Jure Belli et Pacis* (The Law of War and Peace).

These obstacles continue; the documents from the UN Conference on the Law of the Sea have not yet been ratified. The UN General Assembly asked a commission in 1969 to prepare new laws regarding Law of the Sea. In 1982 the work was finished. 160 nations participated in the preparation, but not enough countries have ratified the treaty, and many high-technology nations are among those not ratifying.

As no agreement was reached regarding mining operations in deep international waters, a new commission was set up to review the situation. This commission has succeeded in reaching a general agreement by the UN members in declaring the nodules, the metal deposits found at very great depths in the oceans, *The Common Heritage of Mankind*. This is a sublime decision. The members of the new commission are discussing how to protect the developing nations from their loss of income if the nations having the technical know-how to decide to mine these deep-sea minerals, taking advantage of not having ratified the Law of the Sea, and if they bring these metals on the world market. To date, no law to protect the common heritage of mankind has seen the light of day.   As soon as possible, Outer Space and Antarctica should also be declared our common heritage.

Legislation on the Atmosphere

In 1988, 300 scientists and politicians meeting in Toronto under the UN auspices advised that the discharge of carbon dioxide should be reduced by 20% before the year 2020. This 20% was definitely not enough, according to the scientists, but the politicians considered even 20% as too difficult to obtain agreement on. At the same time they requested that U N institutions should be given the power to enforce any new laws pertaining to this.

Legislation on Space

The Star Wars Project of Ronald Reagan (SDI) could have polluted outer space if the satellites and space installations had broken into splinters. This might have prevented peaceful uses of outer space. NASA in the US has satellites orbiting the world in order to photograph our planet with specially sensitive films. These LANDSAT satellites would be put to better use if they were to locate polluted areas. Now they are mainly used to spot metal deposits in the soil. It does not promote justice on earth when limited numbers of people in the US are informed where in the Third World it would pay to buy real estate, for instance.

Regional Agreements

Regional negotiations to limit pollution are going on in a number of places. The European Common Market is, in addition to many other projects, preparing a proposal for a tax on carbon dioxide emissions. Power stations and companies will have to pay a charge in proportion to their carbon dioxide emission. A charge on petrol is also being discussed, as well as other regulations, dictated by political concerns. The new regulations will probably indicate a minimum level charge. Thus the Danish government will be allowed to introduce a higher charge than, let us say, England or Italy, as long as the Danes can reach agreement at the national level.

In countries around the Baltic Sea, negotiations to establish regional cooperation in environmental regulation are well on their way. These countries have very different ties to established international alliances, but intend to cooperate regionally to safeguard their own internal sea and coastal regions.

The CSCE countries (Cooperation and Security Conference in Europe)

The 34 countries that signed the Helsinki Final Statement of 1975 (all countries in Europe, Canada, US and USSR) ought to be an obvious grouping for legislation on the environment. After the on-going negotiations on disarmament, political co-operation regarding pollution should follow very naturally. The CSCE covers a very large area containing mostly highly industrialized countries, and pollution abatement in this area would be highly beneficial to the whole world.

Decision-making Processes

Future legislative activities will raise high demands on the weighting of votes. The present voting system in the UN, with one vote for each country, whether large or small, rich or poor, cannot constitute the basis of satisfactory decision-making processes.

Voting based on the number of inhabitants in the various countries and modified by other factors, such as wealth/affluence, degree of pollution, number of square kilometers, average life expectancy, will, after being processed in computers, give the background for taxes, charges and rights to consume the products of our planet.

Conclusion

International legislation on environment will require attention from both physical scientists and legal experts. Just as in the field of disarmament verification (see the essay by Douglas Scott in this volume), the enforcement of compliance with environmental treaties will require both types of knowledge (physics/chemistry and law), as well as careful meshing of national and international legislation.

Difficult though this is, action cannot longer be postponed.

About the Authors

Bjø rn Mø ller (age 39), MA in History and Ph.D. in Political Science, since 1985 researcher (now senior research fellow) at the Centre for Peace and Conflict Research in Copenhagen. He is the author of amongst others of following works: *Resolving the Security Dilemma in Europe: The German Debate on Non-Offensive Defense* (London: Brassey's, 1991); *Common Security and Non-Offensive Defense: A Neorealist Perspective* (Boulder, Col.: Lynne Rienner, and London: UCL Press, 1992); and the forthcoming *Alternative Defence Dictionary* (London: Adamantine Press, 1992).

Arnold Simoni has been an engineer and head of his own manufacturing company (electronic equipment) in Toronto, Ontario, Canada. In 1964 he participated with Dr. Norman Alcock (a physicist) in founding the Canadian Peace Research Institute. He produced two books, *Beyond Repair* (1972) and *Crisis and Opportunity* (1983) and several booklets and articles. He now works with the Centre for Strategic Studies at York University, Toronto, on disarmament issues.

Hanna Newcombe was born in Prague, Czechoslovakia, but has been in Canada since 1939. With a Ph.D. in chemistry, she switched to peace research in 1962 and has been the editor of Peace Research Abstracts Journal from 1964 to the present. She was a co-founder of the Canadian Peace Research and Education Association, and is a former President of the World Federalists of Canada and current President of the World Federal Authority Committee. She teaches a peace course at York University (Toronto), and is the author of the book *Design for a Better World* and many articles and book chapters. She is the recipient of the Lentz International Peace Research Award and an Honorary LLD from McMaster University, Hamilton, Ontario.

192

Dietrich Fischer, born 1941 in Switzerland, is an Associate Professor of Computer Science at Pace University in White Plains, New York. From 1976-86 he taught economics at New York University. From 1986-88 he was a MacArthur Fellow in International Peace and Security Studies at Princeton University. He is a board member of Economists Against the Arms Race. He has been a consultant to several United National agencies on questions of disarmament and development. Currently he is writing a book on *Non-Military Aspects of Security: A Systems Approach for the United Nations Institute for Disarmament Research*.

Douglas Scott practised law in Hamilton, Ontario for thirty-two years and retired in 1985 to devote his energies to disarmament. Prior to his retirement, he was active in the Progressive Conservative Party and was elected a trustee of the Hamilton Board of Education in 1960 where he served for two years. He served for many years as the chairman of the Hamilton Branch of the Canadian Institute of International Affairs. Since forming *The Markland Group* in 1987, he has published several articles in newspapers and periodicals, including (as co-author with Walter Dorn) an article in *International Perspectives* (January-February 1989) entitled *Making Arms Control Treaties Stronger*. In 1990, he delivered a paper in Kühlungsborn, Germany entitled *The Concept of Treaty-Mandated Compliance Legislation Under the Biological Weapons Convention* which was published in 1991 by Akademie Verlag.

Walter Dorn is a doctoral student in chemistry, a member of the Markland Group and Science for Peace. He initiated Science for Peace's official contacts with the UN and, for many years, has been their official representative there. His present doctoral work on membrane biophysics is relevant to chemical sensors for the verification of chemical disarmament, and he has twice received the Canadian Institute of International Peace and Security's scholarship in support of his research. His publications include the monograph *Peacekeeping Satellites: the Case for International Surveillance and Verification* (1987) and over two dozen scientific and peace research publications including non-government briefs to the UN and briefs to parliamentary committees. Mr. Dorn is a marathon runner and took part in the lengthy cross-Canada portion of the Sri-Chinmoy Oneness-Home Peace Run.

Finn Seyersted is professor of international law and international organizations at the Institute of Public Law at Oslo University. He was formerly *inter alia* deputy permanent Norwegian representative to the UN 1946-48, Rockefeller fellow 1950-51, expert on mission for UNESCO to Indonesia, Philippines and Laos 1953-54, chief of division, Norwegian Ministry for Foreign Affairs 1955-60, Director Legal Division, International Atomic Energy Agency 1960-65 and ambassador to Argentine, Paraguay and Uruguay 1968-73. He has published works on UN forces in *The Law of Peace and War* (Leiden, 1966) and on the common law of international organizations.

Robert Betchov, Ph.D. in Theoretical Physics from Switzerland is currently Professor Emeritus from Notre Dame University in Indiana, USA and Fellow of the American Physical Society. Now doing peace research in Geneva for the World Federal Authority Committee, mainly on weighted voting in international organizations.

Erika Erdmann, author of *Beyond a World Divided* (with co-author David Stover) has recently retired from her work as library research assistant for Nobel Laureate R.W. Sperry. Independently she conducted a research project *In Search of Values for Human Survival* (published by her advisors, Alan and Hanna Newcombe), on the basis of which she has now been selected to join the International Advisory Board of the World Culture Project (associated with UNESCO). She also publishes Humankind Advancing – a quarterly searching for and promoting the work of persons with the gift to lead humanity toward more responsible, future-oriented thinking.

Charlotte Waterlow graduated from Cambridge University, England in 1936 with First Class honours in history. From 1940-53 she worked in the British Civil Service, dealing in the Foreign Office from 1945-53 with the economic and social developement of the Middle East and the problem of the Palestinian refugees. For this work she was awarded the M.B.E. by George VI. In 1954 she took up high school teaching in the UK until 1967, and in the US from 1970 until 1982, in Cambridge, Massachusetts, where she specialized in teaching 20th century world history at 11th and 12th grades. She has published four textbooks in this field, including *Europe 1945-70* (Prentice Hall and Methuen, UK) and a book on the gulf between the rich and the poor countries, both while living in the US (where she acquired American nationality). After retiring to the UK in 1982, she has been active in the World Federalist Movement, particularly in promoting global structures in the field of environment and development. She has travelled widely in Europe, North America, India, Russia and China.

Digby J. McLaren is past-President of the Royal Society of Canada and an adjunct Professor at the University of Ottawa. He is a member of the Board of the Canadian Global Change Program of the Society. He was Director General of the Geological Survey of Canada and was active in research on the geology of Western and Arctic Canada, global extinctions and asteroid impacts, and global change. Recently he convened and edited the final report of two Dahlem Conferences on Resources and World Development (with B.J. Skinner), and a book on Planet Under Stress (La Terre en Péril) (with Constance Mungall).

Ruth Gunnarsen is a Teacher , Consultant for adult education and Career-Counsellor. At present she is chairperson of

Womens' International League for Peace and Freedom in Copenhagen. She is also a Member of the Council of the Movement for World Federalism and Secretary-General for the World Federal Authority Committee.

Printed and bound in Canada by
Best Gagné Book Manufacturers

9 780888 669506